P9-DMX-189

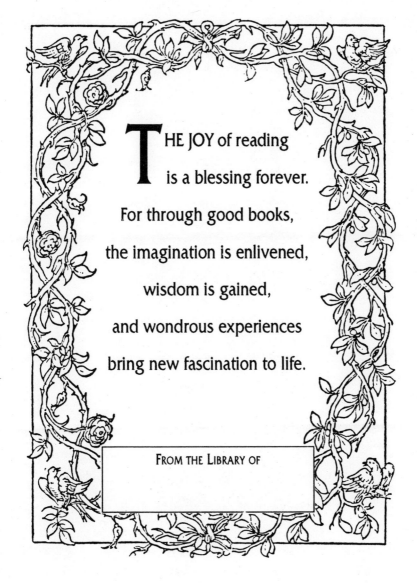

THE JOY of reading
is a blessing forever.
For through good books,
the imagination is enlivened,
wisdom is gained,
and wondrous experiences
bring new fascination to life.

FROM THE LIBRARY OF

The *Art* of FORGIVING

When You Need to Forgive and Don't Know How

LEWIS B. SMEDES

COMPLETE AND UNABRIDGED

CHRISTIAN **Family** BOOK CLUB

Since 1948, The Book Club You Can Trust

Library of Congress Cataloging-in-Publication Data

Smedes, Lewis B.
The art of forgiving / Lewis B. Smedes.
p.   cm.
ISBN 0-345-40412-2
1. Forgiveness—Religious aspects—Christianity.   I. Title.
BV4647.F55S58   1996
234'.5—dc20   95-51543
                                                                                          CIP

First Edition: April 1996

10 9 8 7 6 5 4 3 2 1

First Hard Cover Edition for Christian Family Book Club:1996

"Doing good gracefully is an art."

∾

To
Max and Esther De Pree

Artists

CONTENTS

ACKNOWLEDGMENTS

I want to thank a few special friends for their help in the making of this book.

My agent, Sandra Dijkstra, who first persuaded me, against my doubts, that a new book on forgiveness might be helpful and gently nudged me to keep at it until I got it right.

My editors at Moorings, who led me with sure hands through my literary oddities toward a finished piece that is notably better than the manuscript I first sent to them.

My friend, Dr. Mary Rotzien, who read the first draft of this book (as she has done for me before) and persuaded me that if I worked hard something might come of it after all.

My wife, Doris, who was with me at the start and at the finish of every day's work, a nourishing presence.

My Lord, who is always above, beneath, behind, before, and in me.

For these, and for others unnamed, I am grateful.

Lewis B. Smedes
Sierra Madre, 1996

INTRODUCTION

One of God's better jokes on us was to give us the power to remember the past and leave us no power to undo it. We have all sometimes been willing to trade almost anything for a magic sponge to wipe just a few moments off the tables of time. But whatever the mind can make of the future, it cannot silence a syllable of the past. There is no delete key for reality. And it comforts us little to know that not even God can undo what has been done.

> The Moving Finger writes; and having writ
> Moves on: nor all your Piety nor Wit
> Shall lure it back to cancel half a Line
> Nor all your Tears wash out a Word of it.
> Edward Fitzgerald

It would give us some comfort if we could only forget a past that we cannot change. But the ability to remember becomes an inability to forget when our memory is clogged with pain inflicted by people who did us wrong. If we could only choose to forget the cruelest moments, we could, as time goes on, free ourselves from their pain. But the wrong sticks like a nettle in our memory.

The only way to remove the nettle is with a surgical procedure called forgiveness. It is not as though forgiving were the remedy of choice among other options, less effective but still useful. It is the only remedy.

The remedy has existed since the first wrong done one human being by another. Yet, people still punish themselves with the pains of a past long gone. Or punish others in a futile passion to get revenge. Tribes slaughter tribes, ethnic groups assault other ethnic groups, and gangs shoot up other gangs. Couples break their marriages and divide their families into weeping pieces. All because they will not make use of the one means given to us for recovering from the insults and injuries of a past that never should have been.

Why do people surrender their tomorrows to the unfair pain of their yesterdays? The total answer lies buried somewhere in our primitive need to protect our pride, in our trembling fear of feeling weak, and in our moral instincts for justice, all mingled together as a raw passion to see he who wounded us wounded in equal measure. But I believe that the answer is also tangled in a web of misunderstandings about forgiveness itself.

More than ten years ago, moved by the discovery that forgiving is a gift God has given us for healing ourselves before we are ready to help anyone else, I wrote a book called *Forgive and Forget*. Now, after ten years of further thought and scores of conversations with some of the half million and more people who read the first book, I find there is more to say.

In my earlier book I wanted to motivate people to forgive. In this one I want to answer their questions. In the first book, I wanted to share a discovery. In this one, I want to help people use it more effectively. If the earlier book was for inspiration, this one is for understanding. If the first offered a menu, this one shares the recipe.

Forgiving, when you come down to it, is an art, a practical

art, maybe the most neglected of all the healing arts. It is the art of healing inner wounds inflicted by other people's wrongs.

To do the healing well, we need to know:

what makes it work,
why we do it,
what to forgive and what not to forgive,
how to know when the time is ripe,
whether to resume a relationship again after forgiving,
whether to tell the person we forgive that we've
  done it,
how to know whether we have actually done it, and
  above all,
how to do it right.

We also need to clear up some false notions about forgiving. Like the notion that if we forgive someone we are virtually inviting him to wallop us again. Or that if we forgive what he did we are implying that what happened was not all that bad. Or that if we forgive someone for doing us wrong we are exempting him from the demands of justice. Or that if we forgive we are expected to go back into the old relationship that he ruined.

These are things that every wounded person needs to know when he or she practices the art of forgiving. They are the sorts of things *The Art of Forgiving* is about.

I

WHAT WE DO WHEN WE FORGIVE

One

THE THREE STAGES

Jennifer Klein was the kind of woman you could count on to reach out to a person in trouble. For instance, when Archie, her husband of twelve childless years, came home with a story about this poor kid named Lennie he knew at the shop and how her parents had tossed her out in the street, he sparked Jennifer's inner urge to seek and to save the lost. Without so much as looking up, she said, "We've got an extra room, maybe we can do her some good. Why don't you bring her here?" So he did.

Lennie was only seventeen, nothing fetching to look at, and no joy to have about, mousy and weepy one day, poutish and irritable the next. But her manners only encouraged Jennifer's hunch that she was performing a bona fide Christian service. Care and nurture were what the child needed— unconditional love if you will—and Jennifer felt that she had a calling to give them. *Maybe this was why the Lord never gave me any children of my own to take care of,* she would muse to herself.

Meanwhile, she never worried for a minute about leaving a mere child like Lennie hanging around the house alone with Archie. Well, on a Sunday afternoon, two months after Lennie had moved in, Jennifer strained her thigh while she worked out at her fitness center and came home a half hour earlier than she said she would. When she got there, she found Archie and the castaway in the family room in a compromising prone position.

Jennifer felt she had been mugged inside her soul by a two-ton thug. Is this what a person gets for showing somebody a little tender mercy?

Jennifer wasted no time. She found herself an apartment and left Archie the very next day. Now, two years later, her spirit is still aching and wracked in pain. She still has a hankering to kill the two of them. "Was he up to something even before he brought her home? I don't even know. And me, what a fool I am. I don't know why I set myself up for trouble, me and my idiotic need to be everybody's guardian angel. But he took advantage of me. Dear God, I hate that man so much it's killing me."

And then, without so much as a shift of tone, she dares me to tell her what a person is supposed to do when she needs to forgive somebody: "I've heard it all my life, we should forgive people who slam us. But now when it happens to me, I don't have a clue what it is I am supposed to do."

Somebody had told Jennifer that if she forgave Archie she would put the episode behind her, forget the whole thing, go back to him, accept who he is, and get on with their life together. As if nothing ever happened. But this sounded phony to Jennifer, and she knew she could not do it anyway. "Are you supposed to swallow hard, let him off the hook, and pretend the whole thing never happened? If that is what forgiving is about," Jennifer said, "I would rather buy a gun and shoot them both."

"But whoever told you that had it all wrong, Jennifer. That is not what forgiving is about at all. Not a bit of it."

"All right, so I'm listening. Tell me, what *is* forgiving about?"

Fair question. If forgiving is the only remedy for the pain

of a broken trust, we had better know what it is that a person does when she forgives the one who broke it. We need to know *what* we are supposed to do before we get into the why and whom and when and how to forgive.

Mind you, my business is not to figure out why Archie did what he did. Or to explore Jennifer's compulsion to save the world. And what of Lennie? Must she be forgiven, too? Or will she have to do some forgiving of her own? Probably both, sometime, God knows when. But for just now, we have enough on our hands with Jennifer's simple question: What do we do when we forgive someone?

Is forgiving the same for everyone? Is there a generic forgiving that would be right for Jennifer in her situation and right for the rest of us in our situations? The answer is yes and no.

First the yes. The basics of forgiving are the same for everyone. When we forgive someone, we all perform the same basic transformation inside our inner selves. Each person's healing follows the same basic script. This is why, for all of us, no matter how badly we have been hurt or when or why it happened, the remedy has one name: forgiveness.

Now the no. No two situations are exactly the same. And no two people feel exactly the same way after they have been wronged. Each of us naturally puts her special spin on the inner process of forgiving the wrong. And each of us makes his own decision about how to relate to someone after we forgive her. We all play our own variations on the single forgiveness theme.

Still, the fundamentals are the same for everybody. We all pass through three stages of forgiving. And it is the fundamentals of each stage that I want to run through now. First let me identify them.

We rediscover the humanity of the person who hurt us.

THE ART OF FORGIVING

We surrender our right to get even.

We revise our feelings toward the person we forgive.

Rediscovering the Humanity of the Person Who Hurt Us

I have heard that 80 percent of what we see lies behind our eyes. If this is so, 80 percent of what we see when we look at a person who recently wronged and deeply wounded us must lie behind our eyes in the memory of our pain. We filter the image of our villain through the gauze of our wounded memories, and in the process we alter his reality.

We shrink him to the size of what he did to us; he *becomes* the wrong he did. If he has done something truly horrible, we say things like, "He is no more than an animal." Or, "He is nothing but a cheat." Our "no more thans" and our "nothing buts" knock the humanity out of our enemy. He is no longer a fragile spirit living on the fringes of extinction. He is no longer a confusing mixture of good and evil. He is only, he is totally, the sinner who did us wrong.

As we start on the miracle of forgiving, we begin to see our enemy through a cleaner lens, less smudged by hate. We begin to see a real person, a botched self, no doubt, a hodgepodge of meanness and decency, lies and truths, good and evil that not even the shadows of his soul can wholly hide. We see a bubble held aloft by the blowing of a divine breath. We see a human being created to be a child of God.

Forgiving our enemy does not turn him into a close friend or a promising husband or a trustworthy partner. We do not diminish the wrongness of what he did to us. We do not blind ourselves to the reality that he is perfectly capable of doing it again. But we take him back into our private world as a person who shares our faulty humanity, bruised like us, faulty like us, still thoroughly blamable for what he did to us. Yet, human like us.

Surrendering Our Right to Get Even

After we have been wronged—and wounded in the bargain—been swindled, cheated, abused, or demeaned, no human right seems more sacred than the right to get even with the scab who wronged us. We want to get back at him, make him feel—at the very least—as much pain as he made us feel. Nothing could be fairer. Or taste so sweet. Or seem more deserved. "They're gonna get it," we heard Richard Nixon grumble on his vengeful tapes. I think the ancient Greek poet Homer was smacking his lips when he drooled about revenge. It tastes so sweet, he said, we swirl it around on our tongues and let it drip like honey down our chins.

We want our enemy to suffer, yes, but we also want him to *know* that he is suffering *only* because of what he did to us. We don't want him to admit he made a mistake, flip an apology in our direction like a fifty-cent gratuity, and go on as if he had done nothing worse than burping before dessert. We want the satisfaction of watching him turn and burn with hellish leisure on the rotisserie of his remorse.

As we move along a step or two on the path of forgiving, we hold the right to vengeance in our two hands, take one last longing look at it, and let it spill to the ground like a handful of water. With good riddance.

But take care. When you give up vengeance, make sure you are not giving up on justice. The line between the two is faint, unsteady, and fine.

What is the difference between the two? Vengeance is our own pleasure of seeing someone who hurt us getting it back and then some. Justice, on the other hand, is secured when someone pays a fair penalty for wronging another even if the injured person takes no pleasure in the transaction. Vengeance is personal satisfaction. Justice is moral accounting.

Forgiving surrenders the right to vengeance, it never surrenders the claims of justice. Therein lies a key distinction. After Pope John Paul forgave a man who took a shot at him, a journalist commented: "One forgives in one's heart, in the sight of God, as the pope did, but the criminal still serves his time in Caesar's jail." Very true. Human forgiveness does not do away with human justice. Nor divine justice. Consider the Bible's book of Numbers: "The LORD is slow to anger . . . forgiving iniquity and transgression, but by no means clearing the guilty" (14:18 NRSV).

We sometimes get close to justice. We never bring closure to vengeance. In the exchange of pain the accounts are never balanced. The reason is simple. When I am on the receiving end, the pain you cause me always feels worse to me than the pain I cause you. When I am on the giving end, the pain I cause you never feels as bad to me as the pain you cause me. This is why famous family feuds go on to the third and fourth generation. Vengeance by its nature cannot bring resolution.

And when you get down to it, most of our getting even happens only in our private fantasies. That fact adds a safety catch to vengeance; our opponent feels no pain when we attack him in our dreams. But meanwhile, our fantasies become a catheter dripping a spiritual poison into our systems.

I cannot resist telling my own version of a story that John Irving tells in *Trying to Save Piggy Sneed* about the sweet futility of revenge. It is about how Maggie Mousma tried to get even with Apol Sider. Maggie and Apol attended Cromwell College, a respectable Presbyterian center of evangelical learning in upstate New York. Maggie was wiggling her way toward recognition as a desirable freshperson while Apol swaggered as a seasoned senior with a calling to stimulate the hopes of pretty girls like Maggie.

Apol had walked Maggie home from the library one night and before saying good night, kissed her deeply a few times, leaving her in a delirium of hope. A week or so later he burst in on her and moaned a dreadful confession: He just learned that he had syphilis and that she probably had caught it from him, so she should hustle over to the campus infirmary and get herself some antibiotics before the infection spread too far for cure.

It took a week for Maggie's fear of a horrible death to get the better of her dread of exposure. She showed up the next Monday morning at the student health center. The nurse, who had seen even sillier student tricks than this one in her time, assured her that she could not get syphilis by being kissed and that she was the fifth girl this month who thought she had caught it from the tip of Apol's tongue.

A klutz in communicable diseases, Maggie rated an A+ in retaliation. First she posted urgent messages on the bulletin board at the student commons: APOL SIDER HAS SYPHILIS. Next she put it in the local newspaper, three inches of white space bordered in thick black, with the same message in capital letters: APOL SIDER HAS SYPHILIS. And as the sleepy arrivals walked to the commons early Monday morning their eyes were opened by five bedsheets sewn into a fluttering white banner tied between the Doric columns of the front portico with crimson letters painted three feet high and twenty-five feet across: APOL SIDER HAS SYPHILIS.

The sweetness of having stuck it to him was the closest she had ever gotten to ecstasy. There was one catch. Apol, though wanting in finesse, did have money and good connections at the local airport. Just before halftime at the next football game, a classic biplane rattled over the playing field trailing a bigger than usual banner with the words: MAGGIE MOUSMA HAS A FILTHY DISEASE.

Now what? Hire a hit man?

And what would we get for our efforts if we ever did get

even? We would get just about what we would get if an uncle we all thought was rich died and left us a tax-encumbered, earthquake-cracked, ramshackle monster of a mansion that we can't afford to fix and can't afford to tear down. Surrendering our right to get even is the surrender of a very bad pain in the neck. Imagine poor Atlas surrendering his right to carry the whole world on his back.

Some right. Some surrender.

Revising Our Feelings

Once we have rediscovered our offender's humanity and given up our right to enjoy getting even, we begin to feel new feelings toward him personally. We feel him differently after we see him differently.

What we felt before was simple hate. We may disguise it so we won't have to recognize it in ourselves. But hate is hate no matter how we pass it off. It may be the passive hate that makes us feel good when we hear that bad things have happened to the person who wronged us. Or it may be an aggressive hate screaming for the other person to feel a pain at least the size of ours. Whether passive or aggressive, our hurt left us calling heaven to make bad things happen to the bad person who did bad things to us. That is what hate is.

When we begin to forgive, however, we feel a real though perhaps reluctant wish that some good things might come the weasel's way. At first we just muffle our demands that God make some very bad things happen to him. Then when we hear that he is getting remarried, taking a job in Minneapolis or parts farther west, we may actually feel a nudge to hope for some mildly good things to happen to him. If he comes our way, we will shake his hand and tell him we are glad that he is doing so well. The feeling of good will is likely to be weak and hesitant at the start, and we are almost bound to backslide into malice along the way. But if we feel any stirrings of benevolence inside us, any hint that it will be all right with us if some modest bit of good fortune comes our enemy's way, we can be sure that we are teamed with God in a modest miracle of healing.

ℰ

This is, in its essence, pretty much how I explained forgiving to Jennifer Klein. I do not know if she ever decided to try it. I do know that, if she did forgive, she is even now on her way to healing the wound Archie inflicted on her life. She is walking through the three stages of the forgiving process along with everyone in the world who has forgiven another human being.

She is beginning to see the man who wronged her for what he is—a failed human being, not infinitely different from herself.

She is beginning to break the vengeance addiction, surrendering the misery she once thought would bring her satisfaction.

She is, at last, actually discovering a grace in herself to hope that her enemy may still be given some crumbs off the table of grace to make his life livable.

The three stages of the art of forgiving—restoring humanity to the person who wronged us, surrendering our right to get even, and beginning to bless the person we forgive—are the fundamentals of the healing process. No matter who did the wrong or who does the forgiving, when we forgive, we walk this pathway toward healing inside the wounded places of our own minds.

ℰ

Before we go on to the next chapter, I want to tell you why I began this book by setting out the three stages of forgiveness.

I have discovered that most people who tell me that they cannot forgive a person who wronged them are handicapped by a mistaken understanding of what forgiving is. They would have been helped a lot had they gotten a clear picture of the process at the start. There are problems enough surrounding the particular circumstances of our individual wounds and wrongs without being handicapped with a wrong-headed idea of what we are expected to do about them. So I began the book the way I did because I know that we will have a much better chance at success if we start out together with a shared picture of what forgiving is.

Of course, knowing what we are supposed to do is a fair distance from doing it. You could show me a thousand videotapes of what I am supposed to do when I hit a golf ball, and I might still go on slicing the ball into the woods. I would need some extra help as I approached the tee. It is the same with forgiving. The rest of this book is the "extra help" that we all need.

So I invite you to come along and see what can happen when, insulted and injured by people we trusted, we take up the art of forgiving.

Two

THE SORTS OF
THINGS WE FORGIVE

Forgiving is a remedy for just one kind of pain. We don't use surgery to get rid of every unsightly growth, and we don't use forgiving to heal every unwanted wound. There are wounds for which forgiving is precisely the wrong remedy. Philosopher Miguel de Unamuno was right: "Whoever forgives everything forgives nothing." Scattershot forgiving is wasted forgiving.

I am going to illustrate the sort of situation for which forgiving is meant. It is a black-and-white case, which our own cases seldom are, and an extreme case, worse than most, but all the better to make the point bald and clear.

It is about a biochemist named David who has just lately found the job of his dreams. He is working for a small company doing advanced biotech research related to genetic therapy for what have until now been incurable diseases. The job opens a path to the career he has dreamt of having ever since leaving school, and it gives him the satisfaction of helping people in trouble. And as a bonus, he likes the people he works with.

David has quickly struck up a close friendship with one of them, Frank, a notch higher than David in rank, a year up on him in tenure, but then the company itself is only five years old. David and Frank eat lunch together. On Saturdays they play golf at the country club, a company fringe benefit. Their families barbecue together on Sundays.

Frank has a gangling innocence about him, and he talks about his own personal life as if he and David were best friends who had earned each other's trust a long time ago. One evening, after a few beers, as if to outdo him in the sharing of trust, David tells Frank about a horrible psychological crisis he went through a few years ago. When his wife, Madelaine, learns of the conversation later that evening, she isn't sure it was smart of David to talk so freely.

The next Friday, the CEO calls David into his office. He has learned that David spent three months in a private psychiatric hospital six years ago. He knows that David suffered some serious manic-depressive episodes, that he tried to take his own life once, and that during one manic phase he was arrested for raising a rumpus in a department store credit office. David had obviously lied in his application. The struggling company lives off government agency grants, and it cannot gamble with frail psyches like David's. He is fired.

I have told David's story to highlight four components that are present in every painful situation for which forgiving is the right remedy. If they are not present, forgiving is not the right remedy. If they are present, forgiving is the only remedy.

First, David was hurt by a *person*. It was Frank who did it; it was the CEO who did it; it was not something called the corporation that did it.

Second, David was betrayed by what Frank *did;* Frank may have done what he did because he was a bad egg to begin with, but what injured David was what Frank actually did to him.

Third, David was hurt *seriously;* what happened to David could not be sloughed off with a "Sorry about that."

Fourth, he was not only injured by Frank, he was *wronged,* betrayed, stabbed in the back.

In short, what makes forgiving an appropriate remedy for David's undeserved pain is the fact that a person did something that seriously wounded and wronged him.

Now let us stretch these four components in David's situation into four general rules and see how they tell us what to forgive and what not to forgive.

We forgive persons.

Some of us have been badly wronged by a corporation or by a government or by some other faceless organization. Can we forgive institutions? I do not think so. I think we can only forgive persons. But the link between persons and their organizations can be very close. And when we get hurt by the organization, we are faced with a special challenge should we decide to forgive it.

Susan Baker's son was arrested when police said they found a small stash of marijuana on his person. His arrest would have been small potatoes in any of our large crime-driven cities, nothing for the media to pay any attention to. But the young man's father was James Baker, at the time President Reagan's chief of staff. So when the Bakers' son was booked, the story hit the tabloids, the six o'clock TV news, and most newspapers in America and overseas.

Susan Baker was more than worried for her son and more than miffed at the press. She was outraged. She acknowledged that her son was not above the law and that the police had cause to arrest him. But it wasn't fair to single him out for shaming around the world for no reason except that his father was James Baker. They wronged the son, and they wronged his mother. She fumed, felt helpless. She could not undo the wrong, but she felt that she had to do something about herself before her rage soured her spirit.

"I could," she recalls saying, "stew in my self-righteous anger or I could do things God's way." She opted for God's way, the way of forgiving.

But whom could she forgive? Could she forgive a press corps? Or a non-person called The Media? Or must she find certain real, living, breathing, responsible human beings hiding behind the organizational facade and forgive them? When she decided she should pray for those who had injured her, Mrs. Baker had to locate real people to pray for. This, in fact, was what she did and, in doing it, she discovered that her praying became a catalyst for forgiving them.

Susan Baker published her private story, however, because she wanted to call attention to other mothers with wrongs to forgive the size of craters. She had come to know mothers in violent places who saw their small boys shot in the streets for throwing stones at policemen. Murdered, they were, by officers of the law.

If by some amazing grace these mothers try to forgive, can they forgive a faceless force called the police? Or will they have to forgive a real live officer?

Sometimes governments stamp like elephants on people's backs. But people cannot easily forgive governments. In rare moments of history, a leader may apologize for what his government has done. In August of 1995, for instance, Japan's Prime Minister Tomiichi Murayama gave a "heartfelt apology" for the brutal crimes his country committed during World War II. Such apologies rise like incense above the usual self-righteous arrogance of nations. But can the victims of Japan's aggression forgive the *nation?* Perhaps they can forgive Mr. Murayama. But I do not think they can forgive the Japanese nation.

We have the same problem when we are injured by corporations. Corporations, like governments, can use their impersonal powers to our hurt and sometimes our ruin. Think of companies that knowingly sold asbestos with no warning of its danger, that robbed older employees of their pensions, that cashiered younger ones without cause, or that seduced people to invest their pensions in high-risk ventures that were bound to fail. Can we forgive them?

The problem with forgiving corporations is that they are legal fictions. They do not exist in any flesh-and-blood sense. We talk about them as if they were persons. We say, "General Motors laid off 50,000 assembly line workers." But GM did not lay off anyone. Persons—executives—put people out of work. The company did not fire David; the CEO did.

Forgiving is for persons. David, the tough-luck person whose story began this chapter, was indeed wounded and wronged by his company, but if he finally forgives, he will have to forgive his "friend" Frank and his CEO and let it go at that.

We forgive persons for what they do, not for what they are.

You may have noticed that is is always our trespasses—the bad things we *do,* the sins we *commit*—that we ask God to forgive. When it comes to the sorts of persons we *are,* we most want God simply to love and accept us. It is for the deeds we do that he forgives us.

The same thing is true in our daily traffic with each other. We have no calling to forgive anyone for being a blockhead or for being ugly or lazy or arrogant or sloppy or any of the labels we pin on people to mark them as the sort of people we do not like. We are not called to forgive them for being bad people. We like them, dislike them, accept them, leave them, and sometimes weep over them and try to help them improve on their characters. But we don't forgive them.

People do not wrong us by being liars; they wrong us by lying about us. They do not wrong us by being untrustworthy; they wrong us by betraying our trust. And since forgiveness is only for wrongs people do to us, we can forgive them only for *doing* these wrongs.

Besides, it would be too hard to forgive people for what they are. Most people are too complex and too murky for us to be sure of what we would be forgiving them for. Forgiving is difficult enough. Let us not make it harder than it is. When we have wallowed long enough in our bitterness and have made up our minds to forgive, better to narrow things down to something specific. One thing at a time.

We forgive people who wound us seriously.

David's losses add up to a disaster for him: his job, his income, his reputation, maybe his future mental health. The difference between what David suffered and the normal annoyances we bother each other with along our fretful ways is as big and simple as the difference between the bark of a dog and the bite of a rattler.

We all get in each other's way, step on each other's feelings, say silly, thoughtless, painful things to each other. Pains like these we can put up with. In the plusher language of more elegant times, we bear them with *magnanimity*—the quality of a large spirit. The deep ones we save for forgiving.

But the original wallop is only the beginning of pain. There is a reflex pain that comes hard on the heels of the original blow—the reactive pain of frustrated fury. Fueled by our resentment, our memory tucks this pain in an inside pocket of our spirits where it fattens on our happiness. It becomes a pain that swells in the spirit long after the original injury. This is the pain that forgiving was invented to heal.

David will not get his job back by forgiving Frank. Forgiveness will not pay his bills or jump-start his stalled career. The pain that forgiving can heal is the pain of a wounded memory, the frustrated rage, the soul-choking hate. If these pains of the spirit ever get healed, David will be in better shape to resurrect the energy to recoup his losses. And he will be in better condition to control his impulses to trust people too soon. For now, the point is that forgiving is for the truly serious wounds of life, for the inner pain and boiling resentment brought by the deeper cuts that we cannot ignore when they happen and cannot forget after they have been sliced.

We forgive people for wronging us.

There are pains and then there are wrongful pains. If you are doing time for larceny, you are experiencing pain but you are not experiencing a wrongful pain. If you get lung cancer after smoking three packs a day for twenty years, you will not be feeling wrongful pain. A wife who says she will leave her alcoholic husband if he does not go to AA is not inflicting wrongful pain. But if your friend betrays your trust, the pain you feel is wrongful because you did not have it coming and because it is morally wrong to betray a friend.

I told David's story because the wrong Frank did to David is too blatant for us not to see. David did not suffer the lumps that come with working in a high-risk competitive zone. He suffered betrayal. Frank led David to trust him. Then, knowing full well what he was doing, Frank betrayed the trust. Underlined and in bold caps, and as simple as pudding, Frank's perfidy is the sort of wrong that forgiving was created for.

But sometimes the difference between being pained and being wronged gets fudged. A friend harps at your choice of men and sniffs at your taste in clothes. She calls you at all hours of the night to talk about nothing in particular. She is always late and forever short of cash. To top it off, she borrows your new Honda and crushes a fender. She annoys you and causes you absurd and costly inconveniences, but does she wrong you? She is without doubt a bother too big to bear, and she commits first-degree aggravation almost every day, but you conclude that there is a difference between pains in the neck and betrayers.

Suppose, however, that she tells some secrets you trusted her with, tells them to someone she knew could harm you with them. Being long-suffering with a bungling friend won't cover this one. What she has finally done to you is in the same league with selling you for thirty pieces of silver. She has not only annoyed you; she has betrayed your trust.

We all know that the only bonding agent that holds a personal relationship together is trust. A relationship held together only by a contract is not a personal relationship. A community held together only by force is never a human community. Only trust holds personal relationships—friendship, marriage, family, or a larger community of persons—together.

Trust is both the beauty and the fragility of being human. Our need for trusting relationships is inborn, bred in the bone, part of the human design. To break trust is thus to assault the law of life. It is not only harmful, it is a deep moral wrong.

The wrong is compounded because it saps the violated person of courage to trust anyone again. I have heard of a woman from Central America who had been raped in prison many times by her bestial guards, one after the other. She grinds out her most bitter charge against them: "They have taken away my trust; I can trust no one now." Robbed of the power to trust, she has been stripped of something essential to her humanity.

Now we have the answer to our question: What sorts of things do we forgive? The answer has come down to four sentences:

We forgive *persons,* not institutions.

We forgive persons for *what they do,* not for what they are.

We forgive persons for what they do *to seriously wound us.*

We forgive persons for what they do *to wrong us* when they wound us.

ॐ

Forgiving is not meant for every pain people cause us. Never has been, anymore than Prozac was invented to cure the Monday morning blahs. Forgiving is for the wounds that stab at our souls, for wrongs that we cannot put up with, ever, from anyone. When we forgive people for things that do not need forgiving we dilute the power, spoil the beauty, and interrupt the healing of forgiveness. But when we forgive the things forgiving is for, we copy God's own art.

God is the original, master forgiver. Each time we grope our reluctant way through the minor miracle of forgiving, we are imitating his style. I am not at all sure that any of us would have had imagination enough to see the possibilities in this way to heal the wrongs of this life had he not done it first.

Three

FORGIVING DOES NOT MEAN REUNION

A romantic scenario for forgiving someone who wounded and wronged us would have five scenes that, with infinite variations, might well go something like this.

Scene One

James and Sally are friends, but she wants a closer, more romantic relationship. Sally is eager not to lose him. James persuades Sally to tell him a secret about a mutual friend. She had promised never to tell it, but she gives in. If the wrong person heard it, the friend could be badly hurt.

To complicate things further, James has a hunch that he knows the secret and asks Sally outright if what he suspects about her friend is true. Thus, he hangs her on the horns of a dilemma. If she says no, she lies. If she says she doesn't know, she lies. If she says she does not want to talk about it, she would give her friend away. She is caught. But James promises solemnly that the secret would be safe with him. She is highly motivated to please him anyway, so she tells him.

Scene Two

Sally discovers that James has told. He convinced Sally to violate her friend's trust, and then he violated Sally's trust. She feels spiritually debauched. She knows she cannot go on with him as if it had not happened. They are alienated.

Scene Three

James wakes up to the horrible thing he did and feels terrible about it. He goes to Sally and tells her how sorry he is and promises that he will never trick her again. He begs her to forgive him.

Scene Four

Sally believes James, so she forgives him on the spot and takes his promise on trust.

Scene Five

James is so grateful for Sally's forgiveness, and Sally feels so good about forgiving that they become more than just friends. Reunited, they celebrate the beauty of forgiveness with an embrace of deathless love.

So the curtain falls on a romantic fantasy with an uncertain beginning, a muddled middle, and a dubious ending. Some people dream that true forgiving will always end this happily, and others believe that it is at least supposed to. Their belief is part of a notion that forgiving and reunion are really one and the same thing. But the belief is a befuddled one. Forgiving and reunion are not the same thing; linking them turns forgiving into a needless risk for the forgiving person. The ideal script is not necessarily the best script.

There are three reasons why the popular notion that forgiving and reunion always go together is a major misconception.

Forgiving happens inside the person who does it.

Forgiving is not about reunion.

Forgiving does not obligate us to go back.

Let's take a closer look:

Forgiving happens inside the person who does it.

Forgiving happens, as we have seen, inside our minds and hearts. When we do forgive, we rediscover the frail, failed, bruised humanity of the person we forgive, and we give up our fantasy of revenge. We treat the bounder as a fellow human being and wish him well. All this can happen without giving the matter of restoring the relationship more than a second thought.

Though we welcome the person who hurt us back inside the orbit of people we try to care about, we do not necessarily welcome him back into our special circle of friends and family. We can be friendly, volunteer for the same causes, worship at the same church, and send each other Christmas cards. We can say, "Hello there, how are you, good to see you again," and then say a prayer of thanks that we don't have to live with him. We can weep at her funeral and feel a genuine sadness at her leaving. We can even be happy about the prospect of meeting her in heaven. This is what we call being reconciled, and it is what forgiving in the strict sense is about.

Reunion is something else.

Forgiving is not about reunion.

Some people believe that forgiving and reunion go together like sunshine and warmth or marriage and sex. If two people were married before the rupture, they remarry. If they were close friends before the break, they become close friends again. To them, Sally and James acted out the only forgiving script.

I believe, however, that when a person close to us wrongs us, he throws up two obstacles between us. One of the obstacles is our sense of having been violated, which produces our anger, our hostility, our resentment. This is the obstacle that our forgiving removes. But only the person who wronged us can remove the other obstacle. And he can remove it only by repentance and, if need be, by restitution.

In November of 1990, as the long struggle for freedom in South Africa was reaching its climax, a group of black and white spiritual leaders from almost all the churches in that land met at a hotel outside of a little town called Rustenburg. Some of the leaders represented people who had wounded and wronged blacks. Others represented the people who had been so horribly wounded and wronged. These men and women came together to answer two questions: Could the blacks ever forgive? And could blacks and whites ever be truly united as brothers and sisters?

Desmond Tutu, spiritual leader for many in South Africa, answered for the wounded and the wronged of his beloved country. He gave his answer in a straightforward speech that bears the title "We Forgive You" (published in a collection of Tutu's speeches under the title *The Rainbow People of God,* 1994). Forgive, yes, said Tutu: "The victims of injustice and oppression must be ever ready to forgive." But could there ever be a coming together?

Ah, that is another question. "Those who have wronged [us] must be ready to make what amends they can. . . . If I have stolen your pen, I can't really be contrite when I say, 'Please forgive me' if at the same time I still keep your pen. If I am truly repentant, then I will demonstrate this genuine repentance by returning your pen. Then [reunion], which is always costly, will happen. . . . It can't happen just by saying, 'Let bygones be bygones.' "

We can forgive him if he keeps the pen. We should not be his friend unless he gives it back.

We can see the differences between forgiving and reunion clearly if we look at them both from several sides.

It takes one person to forgive.
It takes two to be reunited.

Forgiving happens inside the wounded person.
Reunion happens in a relationship between people.

We can forgive a person who never says he is sorry.
We cannot be truly reunited unless he is honestly sorry.

We can forgive even if we do not trust the person who
    wronged us once not to wrong us again.
Reunion can happen only if we can trust the person
    who wronged us once not to wrong us again.

Forgiving has no strings attached.
Reunion has several strings attached.

Let us be clear that forgiving and reunion are not the same things; a person can truly forgive and refuse to be reunited.

Some people agree that forgiving is one thing and reunion another but nonetheless believe that once we have forgiven, we are expected to go back to where we were before the rupture.

Forgiving does not obligate us to go back.

I want to say three things that show why this is so.

Reunion is sometimes impossible.

Circumstances may prevent us from being reunited. The person we forgive may not be at all interested in getting back together with us. She may be unable to come back to us; she may have gotten married again, moved away, or died and gone to heaven. Forgiving happens regardless of circumstances; for a reunion, the circumstances have to be right.

Reunion is sometimes harmful.

The former friend we forgive may not be good for us. A former husband may be still addicted to abusing women. A former partner may be a crook—a forgiven crook, but still a crook. Being forgiven does not qualify a person to be a friend, a husband, or a partner. And if he does not qualify, we are better off to walk away and heal ourselves alone.

Reunion may be such a threat that it prevents a wounded person from forgiving.

Here was a seriously religious woman being urged to forgive her former husband after ten years of bruising violence. The elders of her church, male to a man, were pushing on her conscience.

"As a Christian woman, you have a duty to forgive him."

"But I cannot forgive him, not yet, maybe never."

"The apostle Paul says that God helps us do the Christian thing."

"The apostle was never punched in the mouth with a Christian fist."

28

"But it is your duty to take him back."

"Is it my duty to be beaten? If that's forgiveness, you keep it."

The discussion was over. But let's look at the dialogue again.

The woman knew that when the elders told her it was her duty to forgive her husband, they really meant that it was her duty to go back and live with him. And when she said she could not forgive him she really meant that she could not *live with him*. By turning forgiving into an obligation to go back to the same abuse, she was robbed of a chance to heal the wounds that still scar her memory. The surest way to convince some people not to forgive is to tell them that if they forgive, they must go back to the person who wounded them.

~

Forgiving is completed in the mind of the person who forgives. When we forgive we see the person who wounded us as a fellow human being worthy of our love, and in that sense we reconcile ourselves to him.

But being reconciled to him as a human being and embracing him as a partner are two different things, and we should keep them apart. If we have forgiven, we have removed one obstacle to reunion—the wall of our own bitterness. Whether we heal the relationship depends pretty much on the forgiven person.

Four

FORGIVING DOES NOT MEAN RESTORING

All of our human idols fall, sooner or later. Some of them repent. Some of those who repent get forgiven. So far so good. But should they be set back on their pedestals? Should we give them their old jobs back? As usual, the answer is: It all depends.

Easy forgivers sometimes get confused about the difference between forgiving someone and restoring that person to the place he held before he did whatever it was that he needed to be forgiven for. Their confusion grows out of the love and loyalty they had for him before his lapse. They felt such a special attachment to him, felt that his fall somehow diminished them, that they need—for their own sakes as much as for his—to see him back in his trusted slot again.

Let's take the old chestnut of a minister, a beloved Episcopal priest, who violated the trust of some women parishioners who sought him as a present help in their troubles. Their self-esteem had been flattened by their parents, their bosses, and assorted others, but mostly by their husbands. They felt unloved and unlovable and wondered whether they should quit the marriage. They naturally came to their minister instead of a rank-and-file therapist because they admired him and trusted him as they could not trust someone who charged people for his helping hand.

The priest was as much a man of nature as he was a man of God. He was himself not totally satisfied with the way things were at his house, and his quiescent lust was jostled by any good-looking woman's need of his close-at-hand ministry. So he found himself leading his counselees to blend their admiration of a minister of divine love with sympathy for a man in need of human affection. Soon two needy people were sliding down the slippery slope of need to the soft nap of the rector's rug.

But he was not as discreet as he was adorable. The vestry found him out and eventually put him out. He confessed and repented, begged to be forgiven, and hinted at his willingness to stay on the job. The vestry said that forgiveness was the business of his victims; the vestry's business was to do the right thing by the congregation. So he had to go.

Not all the members were so tough. We are Christians, after all, they said, and the dear man is in sackcloth. God has surely forgiven him and welcomed him back to his fold. Should we not do likewise?

The vestry saw through the confusion. Sentimental Christians may confuse forgiving with restoration. But not the vestry. "We will welcome him back," they said, "back to the pew and back to the communion rail. But we do not intend to welcome him back to his old job. Maybe we will someday, later, when he proves himself trustworthy, but not yet. For now, we will forgive but we will not rehire." And there is no contradiction in that.

What the vestry understood is that forgiving is no substitute for common sense. Being forgiven qualifies nobody for any job, let alone the job of speaking for the Lord.

Now and then, a brutish criminal with time in jail to reconsider his past gets born again, becomes a changed person, and even gets forgiven by the very person he wronged.

Some people, with amazing but misdirected grace, believe that when such a criminal is sincere and is forgiven, he should be let loose to walk the streets again. Could they be right? Does the fact that he is forgiven and reborn make him ready for release? Sentimentalists may think so. I do not.

Consider a notorious instance.

On the night of August 10, 1969, Charles Manson's famous "family" of drugged fanatics broke into a Los Angeles home and murdered Rosemary and Leno LaBianca. In an orgy of the bizarre, they carved the word WAR with a knife on Leno LaBianca's body and scrawled on the wall in the LaBiancas' blood the words DEATH TO PIGS. They also scrawled on the refrigerator door, again in blood, the words HELTER SKELTER, from a Beatles song that was meant to announce the coming of chaos. The night before, the same gang had murdered five other people, including the pregnant actress Sharon Tate, at her home in a glitzy area in Los Angeles.

The LaBiancas' daughter, Susan Struthers, came home the same day and discovered her parents' mutilated bodies. The horror of what she saw unhinged her. She suffered a nervous breakdown and was a long time recovering. On her way toward recovery, she experienced a spiritual inner healing. This was the first leg on her new journey.

Meanwhile, Charles (Tex) Watson, reputedly the wildest, most brutal of the murderers, was having a spiritual experience of his own. Watson first spent jail time in San Luis Obispo State Prison in California. There he was born again. Now he is a prisoner at Mule Creek State Prison in Texas where he has gotten married and fathered three children.

After Susan Struthers learned about Watson's conversion, and before he had been moved to Texas, she began to write anonymous letters to him. Then, after writing to him for a year or so and without giving him a clue of her identity, she traveled to San Luis Obispo to meet the man who had so malignantly murdered her parents. She found him. To her, he looked clean and seemed respectful and friendly. After a few visits, she told him who she was, the daughter of the man and woman whose blood was on his hands.

Why did she go? She went, she said, to discover whatever meaning there might be for her own life in the senseless horror that he had inflicted on her. But as Watson persuaded her of his sincerity, she stopped looking for meaning in the past and did what she had to do to find meaning in her future. She held out her hand to Watson and said the impossible words: I forgive you.

Did she really do it? Was it truly possible? Only she knows, and maybe she is not yet sure, but she says she really did, or at least began to do it, and to make my point I will assume that she did. But she did still more. And it is the more that concerns us here.

In 1990, Susan Struthers appeared at a hearing of the parole board and made a plea for Watson's release. For what reason? His remorse, she said, was real; she knew it in her heart. His conversion was sincere, and his character had been redeemed. The murderer was ready to take his place among the free and to harm no person on his way.

There was another witness at the hearing. It was Patti Tate, the younger sister of Sharon Tate, the most famous of Watson's victims. Patti Tate did not come to plead for Watson. She came to demand that he be kept in prison until he died. What drives her, apparently, is not, first of all, the public's safety. What she seems to want is retribution, an even score. And she is sure that the score will not be even until Charles Watson has spent all his years in solitary confinement.

Two victims. One forgives and wants the state to set Watson free. The other refuses to forgive and demands that the state keep him in prison the rest of his natural life. Patti Tate's rationale is clear enough. But what does Susan's forgiveness and Watson's rebirth have to do with the release of her parents' murderer?

The clear and simple answer is that Susan's tender mercy has no bearing at all on how the state should execute its tough justice. It has everything to do with her personal feelings about the man who did such a terrible thing to her parents and to her. It has nothing to do with what the state should do with him.

Charles Watson can qualify for restoration on two conditions. One, that he is indeed not a threat to the people with whom he walks the streets. The other, that he has paid his debt to society. And neither Susan's forgiveness nor his conversion can fulfill these conditions for him.

Susan's forgiving attitude may have opened her eyes to a new and better Watson who is ready to redeem his life in the free world. Patti's hate may blind her to whatever change has come over Watson. Susan is sure that Watson has paid his debt, but she is prejudiced by mercy. Patti is sure that he will never pay enough to even the score, but she is biased by hate.

Others, driven by neither mercy nor hate, will have to assess whether Watson is or is not a threat to people, and they must decide whether he has yet paid a just penalty. A wise judge may ignore Susan's forgiving mercy and Patti's unforgiving need for vengeance. A wise judge may let mercy temper justice but may not let mercy undo it.

∾

In the warm glow of forgiving, we may want to use forgiving as a substitute for prudence and justice. But they belong in different categories.

Forgiving is a personal experience that happens inside one person at a time. What happens to the other person, the one we forgive, is up to him. And whether we restore him to the job or the place in society he had before he betrayed us and before we forgave him depends on reasonable judgments about justice and public safety. If we keep all these things— forgiving and judgment and good sense—in their right places, we can let the miracle of forgiving do its own proper work of healing and leave the restoration of the offender to other practical considerations.

Five

WHO CAN DO IT?

Ivan Karamazov has seen terrible things on his journeys through Russia. Now he has come back and is sitting in a tavern with his younger brother, Alyosha. (The scene is found in Fyodor Dostoevski's *The Brothers Karamazov.*) Ivan feverishly forces his brother to listen to one gruesome tale after another of powerful men torturing innocent children. One of Ivan's stories shall haunt me until I die.

A certain landlord had caught a small peasant boy who was idly throwing small pebbles at his dogs. To teach the peasants to respect his property, the lord forced the boy's mother to watch while he set loose a pack of his vicious dogs on her little son. The dogs tore the child's small body into bloody pieces the way a wolf tears apart a lamb. His mother saw it all. So did Ivan.

Ivan is now spent, he has finished, and is outwardly calm, though inside him burns the question that was, in fact, meant to attack the faith of his believing brother. Everything hangs on the answer—the reality of God, the meaning of life, his own sanity, everything. So he stares hard into Alyosha's eyes as if his believing brother were the only person in the world whom he trusted to answer his question.

"Is there in the whole world a being who would have the right to forgive and could forgive such a man?"

Mind now, he does not ask whether the evil nobleman *deserved* to be forgiven. Good people, sure of their own innocence, do ask whether someone who does very bad things could ever *deserve* to be forgiven—a terrorist, for instance, who bombs a building where children are playing. But Ivan is not troubled by whether a man who does great evil can ever *be* forgiven. He wants to know who on earth or in heaven has the *right* to do the forgiving.

Who indeed? It is human to err, yes, but not to forgive; forgiving is divine. "Who can forgive sins but God?" skeptics asked Jesus.

But we get wounded just as God does, and we need to forgive people just as he does. So Ivan's question to Alyosha is our question, too. Who among us ordinary imperfect mortals has the right to forgive?

Forgiving is not for everybody. It has to be done by the right person or it will not do the work it was invented to do. Forgiving has to be done in the right way and for the right reason and at the right time, and above all by the right person.

So, how about ordinary people like us? How do we learn to perform this radical spiritual surgery? Do only saints qualify? Not at all. To qualify for forgiving we need only to meet three requirements.

We need to bear the wounds ourselves.

We need to know we have been wronged.

We need to have an inner push to forgive.

Let us begin with the simplest qualification: *We must bear the wounds ourselves.*

Our wounds qualify us to forgive the way a broken leg qualifies us for entry to the emergency room. Forgiving is about healing wounds. So only people who bear the pain qualify for forgiving the person who inflicted it. The English poet John Dryden offers the elegant line "Forgiveness to the injured does belong"; it has become an almost absolute rule, as well it should. Forgiving is an affair strictly between a victim and a victimizer. Everyone else should step aside.

That forgiving is something only the injured do is of the essence, and yet educated people persist in getting it wrong. In 1986, Ronald Reagan whipped up a moral storm when he revealed his plans to visit a cemetery in Bitburg, Germany, where Nazi SS troops were buried. As heads of state do, he planned to lay a wreath in their memory. Maybe he meant no more than a generous gesture of sympathy for German mothers whose sons died for their country. "With malice toward none and charity for all"—why not? But when a president lays a wreath on the graves of SS members—the brass knuckles of Hitler's curled fist—he is signaling to the world that all is forgiven.

The trouble was that Reagan was not qualified to forgive a single SS trooper. No one—not a president, not a peasant—has a right to forgive anyone for wounds he himself did not suffer. Charity for the mothers of Nazi sons is fine. But no one but their victims can forgive Nazi sons.

Sometimes, however, our lives are so bonded to the victims that the injuries they suffer wound us, too. The worst wounds I ever felt were the ones people gave to my children. Wrong my kids, you wrong me. And my hurt qualifies me to forgive you. But only for the pain you caused me when you wounded them. My children alone are qualified to forgive you for what you did to them.

Harry Truman never forgave Ike Eisenhower for the wrong he did—in Truman's eyes—to General George Marshall. In the 1952 presidential election, Eisenhower refused to speak out for General Marshall against Joe McCarthy when the Wisconsin senator had called the general a "communist dupe." It was for Truman, in the words of his biographer David McCullough, "an act of unpardonable betrayal" (in *Truman*). Eisenhower had not hurt Truman directly. But Truman was so linked in comradeship to Marshall that what Eisenhower did to Marshall he did to Truman. And when Truman was eighty-seven years old, he told Merle Miller (in *Plain Speaking*) that he had never been able to forgive Ike. As far as we know, he never did. I'm sorry Truman was unable to forgive Eisenhower; my point here is that he would have had the right to forgive him because when Truman's friend was wounded, he was wounded with him.

I want to go back to the question Ivan Karamazov asked his brother Alyosha after he finished his terrible story about the landlord who forced a mother to watch while he set his dogs on her little boy. Ivan demanded to know who could ever have the right to forgive such a man. No one surely, no one in the whole world could do it. Except perhaps one. Would the boy's mother, who was forced to watch it all, would she not have the right to forgive the lord?

Never! Ivan would not hear of it. Not even the mother has the right to forgive the monster for what he did to her child: "If she wants to," Ivan allowed, "she may forgive him for herself, for having caused her infinite suffering. But she has no right to forgive him for what he did to her child."

Who are we, after all, to assign ourselves the role of substitute forgiver? We have no right—no, not even the right to stand in the place of our children and forgive those who have wronged them.

And yet (oh, those two patient words that so vex us when we have just settled down with some simple truths) and yet, there may be a place, now and then, for surrogate forgiving.

Christ once told his disciples that whatever they forgave on earth God would forgive in heaven. An amazing asser-

WHO CAN DO IT?

tion. But why not? When any person forgives another, he or she does what God does. So, if *we* forgive someone who hurt us, why may we not count on it that God forgives him, too? What good does it really do us to forgive people if God is still holding a grudge against them?

But if we can forgive on behalf of God, can we ever forgive someone on behalf of a fellow human being who is not around to do it for himself? Why not? Suppose you injured a person once who is now in heaven (where no one holds a grudge). Suppose I *know* that the person you injured would forgive you if he were here. Wouldn't it be all right for me to forgive you on his behalf, as if he were right there doing it himself?

In a television production of Robert Cormier's story *The Moustache*, a widow named Viola, getting on now, a bit scatterbrained, not always in touch with routine reality, is tortured by one vivid memory of a wrong that she did to her husband, Walter. Her only failing as a wife was her jealousy, and it was her jealousy that led her to hurt the only man she ever loved. She is wrung out with remorse for having done it.

Viola had gotten it into her head that Walter was carrying on with a flirty beauty who worked at his office. Viola nagged him about it, needled him day and night for more than a year, made his life a misery. Then he died, too soon, unexpectedly, leaving Viola alone with her nasty suspicions. Afterward, she learned that nothing at all had been going on, all her suspicions amounted to no more than an insecure wife's fantasies, all false. And Walter died before she could ask him to forgive her.

She knew for certain that she had done him a terrible wrong, accused him most falsely, most unkindly, violated his right to be trusted, and wrecked the last year of his life. Oh, she did repent. Nobody could have felt worse about any wrong. Yet, she would die with a load of unforgiven wrong in her heart unless Walter could somehow tell her that she was forgiven. But Walter was not there to forgive her.

Viola's grandson Jed was visiting her one day at the nursing home and—rattled as she was—Viola thought Jed was Walter. She talked to Walter a long time about the good times they had together early on, and then she heaved her remorse onto her grandson.

"You will never know how much I have regretted what I did, all these years. I am so terribly sorry. Can you ever forgive me, Walter?"

What is a grandson to do?

"Yes, Viola, I forgive you. It's all right; don't worry about it; you are forgiven."

It was spoken like a blessing long longed for from Walter. And it was spoken by a stand-in, a grandson. But Viola heard it as if from the lips of her own husband. She sighed deeply, drooped her muddled head and slipped back into her own muses, at peace with herself and Walter, a forgiven woman. Jed, pinch-hit forgiver, left saying nothing, feeling good.

What really went on between Viola and Walter and Jed? Was it a gentle farce, spiritual make-believe, a forgiveness placebo? I don't think so. Not necessarily. Why could not a grandson—for one moment of substituted grace—stand in for his grandfather and forgive on his behalf?

Nonetheless, exceptions only underscore a general rule that still holds: Only the wounded may forgive those who wound them.

Now the second requirement: *To be a qualified forgiver you must be a wronged person.*

It is one thing to be hurt and another thing to be wronged, and we need an eye for the difference. Some people seem blind to the moral factor of life. They just cannot see it. They are morally handicapped.

Some people tend to be apathetic when someone does

them serious wrong. Others tend to be volcanic when some-one steps on their toes. Both have a failing when it comes to discernment. The first sort put up with the worst of unfair slings that people aim at them, put up with them as if they had them all coming. The second kind spring into action like alarmed leopards in instant retaliation for any accidental inva-sion of their space. The first type puts up with everything. The other puts up with nothing. Neither type does well at forgiving.

Discerning people have an eye for moral differences. When someone hurts them accidentally, they accept it as one of the risks of living around clumsy people. But when they realize that it was no accident, that the person who hurt them knew what he was up to, they know that they were not only wounded, they were wronged besides. This is the kind of moral discernment that qualifies a person for forgiving.

We are wronged if a friend betrays our secrets, or a parent abuses us, or a partner steals from us, or a colleague lies about us and costs us a promotion. We are wronged whenever someone gets us to trust him and then uses our trust to exploit us.

Of course, anybody can be wrong about being wronged. We can be conspirators in our own suffering; we may actu-ally have encouraged the person to take advantage of us. Or we may think the other person meant to injure us when in fact we have been victims of a sheer accident. And if it comes down to it, we may have deserved what he did to us. We may *feel* wronged when in fact we are only wounded.

None of us forgives with 20/20 vision. I suppose that many of us have forgiven somebody who did not really need to be forgiven. And it is probably better to forgive too much than to forgive too little. Grace can afford a bit of overspend-ing.

Still, the rule holds: To qualify as a forgiver, one needs the discernment to know that what she suffered, she suffered unfairly, that she has not just been hurt but offended and wronged as well.

We come now to the third qualification: *We need the inner push to forgive.*

Some people seem born with a bent toward forgiving. They slip into forgiving the way a truckdriver slips into second gear. They don't give it a thought; they make their move, and it's done. Even when coping with monstrous betrayal, they seem blessed with natural forgiving talents. They forgive without thinking about it, and then afterward, if they recall how hurt they had been and how they got over it, they may say to themselves, "Oh, I must have forgiven him without even knowing that I had done it."

But few of us are naturals at this game. We don't seem to be born with the forgiveness gift. We need to work at it the way a duffer needs to keep practicing his tee shots. I have known people who believed they were born with a special handicap, temperamentally unsuited, without any potential for performing the smallest miracle. One man told me that his inner forgiver had been broken in childhood and could not be fixed. I told him that mine was broken, too, and that, as far as I knew, there is not a forgiver in the world that is in good repair.

Some of my Christian friends wonder whether "unbelievers" have the inner push needed to forgive someone who stung them badly. I understand their question. Forgiving is the key to the entire Christian agenda. Christ himself said that if we don't forgive people what they do to us, we cannot expect God to forgive us for what we do to him. And did he not himself forgive just about every sorry sinner who came his way, on the spot, no questions asked? Christians certainly have strong motives for trying harder. But does this mean that only Christians can forgive?

I do not think so. I have now and then known people who

did not share my faith but who acted the way I should act if I were a better Christian. They seem to be better at forgiving than I am. When I watch them, I am glad that the energy of God's forgiving spirit spills over into the spirits of people who don't know or care about him as I do.

I have also noticed that some Christians seem to take pride in their meanness. They are hostile to people whose only fault is walking a different walk than they walk and talking a different talk than they talk. For them, hating their enemies appears to be a manly virtue and forgiving them a wimpish vice.

So I choose not to worry about whether other people are less qualified to forgive than I am. It is hard enough for me to do it. Why should I bother my head about whether others can do it as well as I can?

The long and short of it, however, is that in order to forgive, we need to feel an inner push to forgive. We probably won't do much forgiving unless something inside of us makes us want to do it. I am certain that people never forgive because they believe they have an obligation to do it or because someone told them to do it. Forgiveness has to come from inside as a desire of the heart. *Wanting to* is the steam that pushes the forgiving engine.

We forgive when we feel a strong wish to be free from the pain that glues us to a bruised moment of the past. We forgive when we want to overcome the resentment that separates us from the person who wounded us. We forgive when we feel God's Spirit nudging us with an impulse to pull ourselves out of the sludge of our disabling resentment. We forgive when we are ready to move toward a future unshackled from a painful past we cannot undo.

Where does the desire to forgive come from? I believe that every ordinary human desire to redeem the past comes from God, the source of all redeeming graces. So one way to get the desire is to be in touch with God. The hitch is that if we do not want it, we are not likely to ask for it. But we are double-minded creatures. We all know what it is like to ferociously want something at one level and fearfully not want it at another level. And the odd thing is that sometimes the more we want something, the more we abhor the thought of having it. It is often this way with forgiving.

When we get obsessed with what someone did to us, when we cannot get it out of our minds night or day, when our rage churns to a froth, and, in short, when we feel most miserable, we swear that we would not forgive someone if he came crawling on his belly. But as we discover that the resentment that tasted sweet for breakfast is bitter fare for dinner, we begin to wonder whether we shall ever be happy again. And we begin to feel a wisp of a desire to get rid of the sour after-taste of hate.

It is at this precious moment when we begin to think that perhaps we really do, after all, want healing, that we should quickly pray for more of the desire that has already begun to nudge us. Once we begin to pray, our prayer may stimulate our desire for what we pray for. And God will give that desire a shove.

In sum, then, we are qualified to forgive if we meet these three requirements:

We were wounded.

We were wronged.

We have a desire to forgive.

This is all we know and all we need to know about our qualifications for forgiving. I have not said that if we are qualified to forgive we will have an easy job of it. All I have said is that we have a license to practice.

II

WHY WE FORGIVE

Six

THE CASE AGAINST FORGIVING

Sometimes forgiving seems like exactly the wrong thing, even a bad thing, to do. In fact, there are profound thinkers who say that—as a regular way to deal with monsters who do very bad things to people—forgiving can be precisely the wrong thing to do. Their objection is fiercely moral. It is not that forgiving is just too hard for victims to do. Nor even that forgiving is a foolish thing to do. It is that forgiving bad people can be morally wrong.

When people whom I admire tell me that something I recommend could be both dangerous and immoral, I stop and listen. And I have never been stopped and forced to listen as I was when I read Simon Wiesenthal's stunning story in *The Sunflower*. It is the story of how he walked away and left a young SS trooper to die unforgiven when he was in the concentration camp in Mauthausen, Austria. The soldier lay dying from head wounds and begged Wiesenthal to forgive him. But Wiesenthal walked away.

Wiesenthal was a young architect at the time, sure that he was doomed along with the other Jews caught in Hitler's death machine. On a certain afternoon, he was given the job of cleaning out rubbish from an improvised hospital outside the camp where wounded German soldiers were trucked in from the Russian front. Getting toward evening, a nurse took him by the arm and brought him to the bedside of a boyish storm trooper named Karl, whose head was bandaged with pus-soaked bandages. He would soon die.

Karl grabbed Wiesenthal's wrist. He whispered that he had to talk to a Jew, any Jew, before he died so that he could confess some terrible things that he had done to Jews and be forgiven for them. He confessed what he had done while he was stationed in a Russian village named Dnepropetrovsk. His company was ordered to take reprisals in the village. They packed a frame house with Jews, including many children, poured gasoline on the floors, locked the doors, and set the house on fire. People near the windows jumped. The soldiers shot them before they landed on the ground, shot the little children right along with the parents, machine-gunned them in the air as they fell. Karl finished, appeared to be weeping, and then, when he got control of himself, he begged Wiesenthal to forgive him. He could not die in peace unless a Jew forgave him for the terrible thing he did in Dnepropetrovsk.

Wiesenthal listened, awestruck, to everything Karl told him. He said nothing. Finally he yanked his hand away and left Karl to die with his unforgivable sins unforgiven.

Afterward Wiesenthal worried that maybe he had been wrong not to forgive a young man who begged for forgiveness on his deathbed. When the war was over, and Wiesenthal had survived the Holocaust, he wrote his story. At the end of it he asked his readers, "Was my silence at the bedside of the dying Nazi right or wrong? This is a profound moral question that challenges the conscience. . . . What would you have done?"

When I visited the camp at Mauthausen I tried to visualize where Wiesenthal was standing when he decided to leave Karl with his horrible sin unforgiven. I imagined that I was there and that he had asked me whether he had done the right thing. And I wondered how I would have answered him. I have required my students to read *The Sunflower* and compelled them to answer Wiesenthal's question for themselves. I knew that many of them felt called to the ministry to urge forgiveness on people. Now I asked them to consider the possibility that the most typically Christian act—forgiving—could be morally wrong.

The publisher of *The Sunflower* arranged for several distinguished people from many walks of life to write their answers to Wiesenthal's question and published them along with the story. Most of them believed that it was right and good for Wiesenthal not to forgive Karl. Some went further and said that he would have done a very bad thing had he forgiven the dying SS trooper. Most admitted that they did not know what they would have done had they been in Wiesenthal's place, and some were not sure whether what he did was right or wrong.

If you assume that anyone with a bit of mercy in her heart would think that Wiesenthal should have forgiven Karl, read these samples from what several distinguished men and women said to Wiesenthal.

> "You would never have been able to live with yourself had you forgiven him."
>
> "I would have strangled him."
>
> "We cannot forgive murderers."
>
> "I believe you followed a proper and honest path. . . ."
>
> "To forgive everything means that one is lacking in discrimination, in true feeling, in reasonableness, in memory. . . ."
>
> "One cannot and should not go around happily killing and torturing and then, when the moment has come, simply ask and receive forgiving."

"I believe that the easy forgiving of such crimes perpetuates the evil it wants to alleviate."

When my students and I read these sentences together, we sensed that the writers shared two different reasons for their belief that Wiesenthal had done the right thing when he refused to forgive the SS trooper. The first reason was that no one has a right to forgive someone unless he himself had been injured by that person. The second reason was that Karl's crime was too horrible to be forgiven by anyone.

Most of us agreed with the first reason. Wiesenthal, they said, had no right to forgive Karl for what he had done to other people. Only his victims had a right to forgive him. And they were dead. We concluded that if Wiesenthal forgave Karl it would have to be for wrongs that Wiesenthal himself had somehow suffered with the victims as a fellow Jew.

We had a harder time with their second reason, the one having to do with the horror and the depth of Karl's crime. Karl had taken part in the murder of many men, women, and children, all of them innocent. To forgive such wrongs, the writers believed, would destabilize the deepest moral law of the universe. It would violate the deepest moral impulse within a human being. Only a sentimental and amoral fool would forgive such a man.

The moral objection to forgiving rises from our moral instinct for fairness. Forgiving, the writers contended, glosses over the enormity of evil and stifles the call from the bowels of the earth for just vengeance. It treats heinous crime with the same sentiment that it treats a trifling personal offense. Forgiving monsters shrinks great evil to the level of a trivial sin that one can forgive and forget without a second thought.

And then there is the principle of *quid pro quo,* a tooth for a tooth, giving back as much as you get—a law etched deep on every human heart. Forgiving, the critics say, ignores this moral and spiritual impulse. It tempers justice, not with mercy, but with folly. If forgiving sounds to us like mercy to a penitent person, let us remember that it tells evil people ahead of time that no matter how many people they hurt and kill, forgiveness will be waiting for them at the front door.

But there are still more arguments against forgiving.

Forgiving is wrong, some argue, because it is *dishonest*. In the name of a cruel kindness, it denies reality. The reality is that someone wronged another human being. Forgiving makes believe it did not really happen. Let a Nazi storm trooper shoot innocent Jews. Let a bully beat his wife. Let a mother abandon her children. Let a friend betray a friend. We will sweep it all under the magic carpet called forgiving and pretend it never happened.

Finally, some critics say, forgiving is wrong because it *contradicts human nature*. Our nature is to get even. Forgiving may be divine, but what is natural to human beings is to pin the abusers of the world to the floor and make them pay. Pain for pain. Getting even is natural. Forgiving is unnatural.

My students and I wrestled hard with all of these disturbing doubts. Were we perhaps wrong to believe that, in a world where bad people take advantage of good people's kindness, it is forgiving and not vengeance that buys the ticket to a better future? At the end of our conversation, we faced up to the same question that Simon Wiesenthal had asked the others: What would you have done?

I pushed each of my students to give his or her immediate answer, without second thoughts, allowing for all their self-doubts. Most of them were not sure what they would have done had they been in his place. At the end they turned on me and demanded that I answer Wiesenthal's question for myself: What would I have done? This is what I told them.

I said that I could not be sure what I would have done had I stood at Karl's dying bed and listened to him beg me to forgive him. I feared that I might have forgiven Karl all right, but for wrong reasons. I might have forgiven him just to make dying a little more comfortable for him; he was, after all, hardly more than a boy. I feared that I might forgive him because I would not be at peace with the memory of refusing to forgive a dying man. In short, I feared I would have spoken forgiving words just to protect my own conscience.

I hoped, however, that I would have had the wisdom to tell Karl that I had no right to forgive him on behalf of the people he murdered. But I also hoped I would have had faith to invite him to join me in asking God to forgive him.

Why bring in God? It was not God; it was the human Jews whom he shot. Ah, but when he murdered the children of Dnepropetrovsk, he "murdered" God with them. The difference is that God can survive his own murder and live to forgive the person who cut his throat.

But some of my students would not let me talk only of forgiving Karl for murdering other people's children. What, they asked me, if the children Karl murdered had been my own children? Or the children of my children? What would I have done then?

I did not then and still do not know what I would have done if Karl had shot my own children as they tried to leap from a burning house. I know that I would have wanted to strangle him then and there on his deathbed and push him feet first into hell. On the other hand, perhaps I would have been struck dumb by my own doubt, as Wiesenthal was. Perhaps I would have pulled my arm loose from his grip and walked away in silence, not out of conviction, but out of confusion.

Then again, who can know for sure? I might have had the grace to forgive Karl for murdering my own children and then leave him to the judgment and mercies of God. I hope so.

Seven

IN DEFENSE OF
FORGIVING

We know the charges critics have leveled against forgiving—that forgiving makes things unfair, that it is
dishonest, and that it goes against human nature. I shall reply
that forgiving offers the best hope of creating a new fairness
out of past unfairness. I shall respond to the challenge that it
is dishonest by saying that forgiving cannot happen without
severe truthfulness. And to the charge that forgiving goes
against the grain of human nature, I shall say that forgiving
follows the impulses of our true and better natures.

All three criticisms, I believe, are based on a few mistaken
conceptions of what forgiving is about. So before answering
the critics, I want to clear up these stubborn distortions of
the meaning of forgiving. The only way for me to do this
quickly will be to post some simple statements of what forgiving is *not* about:

**Forgiving someone who did us wrong does not
mean that we tolerate the wrong he did.**

**Forgiving does not mean that we want to forget
what happened.**

Forgiving does not mean that we excuse the person who did it.

Forgiving does not mean that we take the edge off the evil of what was done to us.

Forgiving does not mean that we surrender our right to justice.

Forgiving does not mean that we invite someone who hurt us once to hurt us again.

Almost every argument against forgiving assumes that forgiving means what in fact it does not mean. What I will say in defense of forgiving assumes that forgiving is not the sort of thing its critics assume it to be. But now, moving on from assumptions, I want to defend forgiving against the three explicit criticisms that I have mentioned.

Forgiving is fair.

The most important of the three complaints against forgiving is that forgiving is unfair. Forgiving is unfair on the face of it, so goes the claim, because it lets the offender off free and offers nothing to the victim except the risk of more pain. It is unfair to the victim of today and unfair to the potential victims of tomorrow.

The charge is false. The fact is that forgiving is the only way for any fairness to rise from the ashes of unfairness.

The only alternative to forgiving perpetuates unfairness.

I learned long ago that whenever we have to get out of a tough dilemma, the first thing we should do is review our options. There are only two genuine options for responding to a personal injury that we did not deserve. One of them is vengeance. The other is forgiving. Any other way of responding is really a denial. Forgetting, excusing, or overlooking the wrong that was done are all devices of denial that prevent real forgiving from happening.

Vengeance is the only alternative to forgiving. It is, simply put, a passion to get even. We have been unfairly hurt. Life is out of whack. The scales are unbalanced. The only way to balance them and get life back to normal is to inflict as much pain on our abuser as he inflicted on us. An eye for an eye, wound for wound, insult for insult. Revenge—the ancient formula for undying futility.

The reason getting even does not make life fairer is that it never happens. Cannot happen. Ever. Not a chance of it. Will the Tutsis ever get even with the Hutus? Will the Bosnian Muslims ever get even with the Serbs? Will the Bloods ever get even with the Crips on the streets of Los Angeles? Never. They may go on killing each other until they are all dead, but they will never get even. The bodies broken and blood spilled in the futile fight to even the score mock the rationality of the human race.

The reason we cannot get even is that the victim and the victimizer never weigh pain on the same scale. One of us is always behind in the exchange of pain. If we have to get even, we are doomed to exchange wound for wound, blood for blood, pain for pain forever. Perpetual pain. Perpetual unfairness.

Forgiving gives future fairness a chance.

Remember that forgiving is a remedy for an unfairness that has already happened. Someone has been wronged. What happened is unfair and will never be fair. Not even God can make something fair out of what is intrinsically unfair. Only one thing can be done. Something must break through the crust of unfairness and create a chance for a new fairness. Only forgiveness can make the breakthrough.

It gives no guarantee that the forgiver and the forgiven can make things more fair between them. But it opens the window of opportunity. We know for certain that vengeance always makes things even more unfair than they were. Forgiving *always* opens the future to better possibilities. Only a fanatic for vengeance can fail to see that a possibility for fairness is better than the certainty of futility.

Now remember that forgiving does not balance the scales anymore than revenge does. One person or one group will end up having suffered more pain than the other. We know that. But if we step away from where we are, get a clearer view of the flawed humanity of the person who hurt us, and perhaps even grumble a qualified prayer for his welfare, we can make one unsteady step away from our unfair yesterday and point ourselves in the direction of more fairness between us tomorrow.

The charge of unfairness is concerned mostly with the person who has been unfairly injured. Can it be fair to the victim if she gives up her right to get even and even wishes her victimizer well? The answer is that forgiving is the only way for a victim to be fair to herself.

Every victim moves through three stages of unfair pain. The first stage is the original wallop. The second stage is remembering the wrong that happened. The third stage is the vengeance stage, the futility of wishing at least equal pain on the person who gave her pain. If the victim allows herself to get mired in the third stage, she will allow the person who hurt her once to go on abusing her in her memory until she dies. Some fairness.

Forgiving is the only way for the victim to stop the grinding wheel of unfairness to herself. It is the only way to move beyond the lingering pains of a past she will not allow to die. The only way to escape the unfairness of her bondage to a bad past. This is why I have said a thousand times that the first and sometimes only person to get the benefits of forgiving is the person who does the forgiving.

I have said what needed to be said about the charge that forgiving is unfair. Now I want to answer the second charge—that forgiving is dishonest. The fact is that:

Forgiving is a severe honesty.

Of course, anybody can lie *about* forgiving. We can use the *words* of forgiving as falsely as we can the words of love. We can say "I love you" and mean "I want to use you." We can say "I forgive you" and mean "I want you to know that you are scum and that I am a better person than you are."

But this is not the sort of lie the critics have in mind. They do not mean that people are not sincere when they *say* they forgive. They mean that fundamentally forgiving is dishonest.

Forgiving, they say, falsifies reality. When we forgive we act as if the rotten thing that happened did not really happen. Or the badness of what happened is not as bad as it was. Forgiving, they say, is a pious form of self-deception.

It is a damning accusation. If forgiving were a sentimental trick to conceal or disguise reality, it would be better wiped off the human agenda. But, thank God, it is neither a pious lie nor a benign deception. It is the one truthful action that bears any chance of healing the wounds of a world hacked apart by memories of wounds and wrongs we know we did not deserve. Let me count the ways of its honesty.

Forgiving is honest about what happened. We forgive only because we have admitted that what was done was an evil thing that has no place in the infinite repertoire of permissible human behavior. Forgiving tolerates no disguising, no denying, no diminishing, and no ignoring of what happened. Forgiving looks the incident full in the face and calls it what it is, a wrong for which there is not a fitting place on God's earth.

Forgiving is honest about the responsibility of the person who committed the wrong. If we do not hold him responsible we do not forgive him. We have other ways of dealing with people who do evil accidentally or in innocent insanity. We forgive only if we know that the person we forgive could have chosen not to do what he or she did.

Forgiving is honest about the accountability of the person who did it. Forgiving does not abolish judgment. Forgiving does not let people off the hook of justice. It frees an offender from our private demand for vengeance; it holds him to the full measure of justice.

Forgiving is honest about the price of any reunion. I may forgive you in my heart and free myself from my hatred of you, but before I rejoin you as my friend, I demand a price from you. The price is honesty. The currency of honesty is remorse and conversion. And there is no reunion unless the price is paid.

Forgiving is honest about the person who wounded us. In our rage we make him out to be only and wholly a swine or a devil. Forgiving restores to the failed and guilty and weak person his own godlike humanity.

Forgiving requires honesty with ourselves. No one can forgive another except he be aware of his own need to be forgiven. In our anger at being wronged, we feel nobly self-righteous. But just as there is more to the person who injures us than his guilt for doing it, there is more to us than the fact of painful innocence. We too are failed and flawed and beautiful.

Finally, forgiving is honest about future possibilities. If we chain our spirits forever to an evil past, we deny the possibility of a better future. If we lock the door to reconciliation and melt the key, we deny the future we deserve to have. The truth about the future is that it carries a possibility—only a possibility but at least a possibility—of a new beginning that can be created from the shambles of an old and evil and unforgotten past. Forgiving is true to the future.

In view of all these facts about forgiving, I submit that there is never any real forgiving at all unless it first be honest.

Forgiving is natural.

The complaint is that forgiving violates our native human impulses. Vengeance, they say, is natural: Everyone has a natural instinct for getting even, a drive to settle scores, a primeval push to hit back. Forgiving stifles this natural instinct and saddles us with an unnatural sentiment that stifles our natural impulses. This, in a nutshell, is the contention.

In reality, however, forgiving expresses our true and best natures.

If it is human to be free for the future, unshackled to pasts we cannot change, then forgiving is natural. If it is human to create new paths out of old ruts, forgiving is natural. If it is human to see beyond what was to what can be, forgiving is natural. If it is human to want to heal our unfair pain and make things fairer than they are, forgiving is natural. Forgiving is contrary to human nature only if it is truly human to follow a blind animal instinct for prolonging unfairness and the pain that goes with it.

Odd thing. We have gotten so used to the things that violate our humanity that we have come to think that they belong to our humanity.

Was it contrary to human nature when South Africa's Nelson Mandela decided that reconciliation and not retaliation was the way out of the petrified unfairness of apartheid? Did he violate human nature when, rather than plunge his nation into the perdition of vengeance, he chose to surrender the right to get even and instead move on to create a new and nobler society out of the dust and ashes of the old unfairness?

Is not Mandela's way in fact one of our century's clearest models of what human nature can be?

As I write, 850,000 Hutu people are living in unbearable squalor outside of Goma in Zaire, almost a thousand of them dying daily from cholera and dysentery, while a good day or two's walk could bring them back to their homes in one of the more beautiful and fertile, even lush areas of all Africa. Why are they away from home, infested with lice, carrying their emaciated, sick, and starving babies to almost certain death? Why must they die and leave orphaned children and stooping elders to die after them?

They suffer because they are enslaved to their wounded tribal memories. The Hutus are slaves of their memories of Tutsi unfairness. Their hate drove them to slaughter a million people in a few months' time. Now the Tutsis are in control of Rwanda. And the Hutus are afraid they will seek revenge. So they die in the desert instead.

Is this human nature? Or is this a fall from nature? Not nature's truth but nature's ruin? I believe that when we break into the cycle of unfair pain and forgive the person who created it, we are following our truest human impulse. If forgiving feels unnatural to us, perhaps it is because in our anger we lose temporary touch with a vital area of our humanity—a loss that grace can nicely replace. To heal the wounded memory is as natural to the human spirit as it is for the cells of the human body to heal themselves.

The old saw has it only half right: To err is human, and to forgive is more human still.

∾

The heart of my answer to the complaint against forgiving is that forgiving is the only way to get ourselves free from the trap of persistent and unfair pain. Far from being unfair, it is the only way for a victim to be fair to himself or herself. Far from being a dishonest denial of reality, forgiving is not even possible unless we own the painful truth of what happened to us. Far from being alien to our human nature, forgiving dances to the melody of our true humanity.

Eight

BECAUSE IT SUITS US

S ome people believe that we do only the things we really want to do. They believe we do what we do because we think doing it will reward us more than if we do something else. Increase your pleasure and avoid your pain—this is the motivation for all human action. No matter how much people talk about doing the right thing simply because it is the right thing to do, we all end up doing what we think will give us more pleasure and less pain. Some people, I say, believe this. I do not believe it.

I believe that we sometimes—not always, but sometimes—do the right thing even if we know that it will cost us a lot of pain. We do what is right simply because we believe it is right. You can even say that the quality of our lives is measured by our willingness to do the right thing—even when we know it will make us pay dearly.

On the other hand, some things are just not meant to be done simply because it is our duty to do them. Some things are meant to be done only because we want to do them. Some can be done for no other reason. If we are not led to do them by our own inner impulses, they won't get done at all. Or at least they will not get done well. Forgiving is one of these things.

It is a safe bet that nobody has ever forgiven anyone because he or she felt obligated to do it. Consider God for a moment. Does God forgive us because he is pressed by some law that obligates him to forgive? Or does he forgive because something inside bends him toward grace instead of revenge? The answer is built into the question. God is not obligated by anything outside his own heart. He forgives because he wants to. And he wants to because he knows that the possibilities for the future are much brighter for both of us if he says yes to forgiving.

Of course, we can push ourselves through the mechanics of forgiving even if it is not what we want to do. A child will grudgingly say she forgives her big brother because her mother insisted she do it. A religious woman may go back to an abusive husband because she believes God commands her to go back. But do they really forgive? I don't think so. Forgiving is an event inside a heart that hurts, and it happens only when we don't want to hurt anymore.

Still, many of us feel that we *ought* to forgive people who injure us. The New Testament Gospels make it clear enough that even if our instincts rebel, we ought to forgive. How do we explain this tension between doing what we ought to do and doing what we want to do?

I think we will resolve the tension when we recall that there are actually *three kinds of ought*.

First, there is an ought of *obligation*. For instance: "You ought to pay your income tax." This ought comes from authority. God has authority. So does the government. When God and government tell us what to do, they expect us to feel obligated to do it. But nobody forgives out of obedience to authority any more than she breathes and thinks and falls in love out of obedience to authority.

Second, there is an ought we should follow because we will be better off for doing it. Call it an ought of *opportunity*. For instance: "You really ought to invest in a retirement plan." We ought to do such things, not because there is a rule that pins us down, but because doing it is an advantage for us and for people we care about.

Third, there is an ought that comes from being the kinds of people we are. Call it an ought of *fit*. We ought to do what suits our sort. We ought to use our heads because we are rational persons. We ought to fall in love because we are loving persons. And we ought to forgive if we are forgiven persons.

Forgiving is an ought of opportunity.

I think that when God says we ought to forgive, he intends something like this: "I have discovered a better way to deal with your memory of wrongful pain. It is an opportunity to do yourself a world of good. It will also put you in shape to do some good for the clod who hurt you and for a lot of other people besides. I call it forgiving. You really *ought* to try it."

The alternative to forgiving—getting even—only makes the pain last longer and feel worse. Even if we cause our enemy the worst pain we can think of, we don't feel any better for it. A sip of sweet revenge, maybe, but with no lasting joy in it. So forgiving is an opportunity to do something beneficial for ourselves and for other people in the bargain.

We also ought to forgive because it suits us.

We do a lot of wonderful things simply because they fit the sorts of people we are. They suit us the way making music suits a lyrical spirit. Birds ought to sing and buds ought to blossom and children ought to dance just because it is in them to do it. Forgiving suits us. It matches our condition as imperfect beings grateful for having been forgiven by others—and by God.

A forgiven person ought to forgive the way a groom ought to be happy, the way a grieving person ought to cry, and a person who has been given much ought to give some away. It just fits.

This is why people do good things. If your heart is right, you will do what is right. If you feel grateful for love given to you, you will be generous in giving love. There will be a fit—a congruence—between what you are and what you feel and what you do.

One day a righteous man named Simon invited Jesus to a dinner party. Jesus came. The dinner had hardly been put on the table when a woman of the night crashed the party, walked right in as if she lived there. She plunked herself down in front of Jesus and began to weep. Then she took his bare feet in her hands, bathed them in her tears, and dried them with the same lush waterfall of black hair that had lured many wandering men to her boudoir. As her *pièce de résistance,* she rubbed his feet with an exotic ointment that she had been saving for a very special occasion.

Simon was floored. How dare she? For that matter, how dare the rabbi play along with her? He must have known the woman was a strumpet. Yet he sat there as a guest in the house of a man with a prime reputation while the prostitute massaged his feet. What was worse, he seemed to enjoy it.

Jesus seized the moment to make one of the most important points he ever made about love and life: Our ability to love is proportionate to our feeling of gratitude about life. If someone feels the joy of having been given much, she is capable of loving much. If one knows she has been *forgiven* much, she loves spectacularly. This woman had felt so guilty and so shamed that when she tasted the grace of forgiveness, she erupted with love like a gusher.

The righteous people around her had convinced her that

she was nothing but a prostitute. God saw and persuaded her that she was a beautiful child of God who was also a prostitute. She discovered that God had surrendered any right to punish her and that he, the maker of the universe, wanted to bless her. In short, she discovered that she was a forgiven human being. And this is why the outlandish thing she did suited her to a T.

This is what I mean by the "ought of fit." We ought to forgive the way a spouse ought to make love, a sad person ought to cry, a happy person ought to smile, a lyrical person ought to sing, and a grateful person ought to say thank you. We ought to do it because it suits us so well.

∾

Everything I have said in this chapter comes down to two simple sentences. We forgive when we discover that we really want to forgive, and we want to forgive when we want to heal ourselves from the hangover of a wounded past. And when we actually do forgive, we are only doing what comes naturally to anyone who has felt the breath of forgiving love on her own heart.

Nine

FOR OUR OWN SAKES

I used to think of forgiving as mercy's way to do something good to someone who had done something bad to us. Then I discovered that the first and sometimes the only person who benefits from forgiving is the person who does the forgiving. I was so moved by this discovery that I wrote a book about it called *Forgive and Forget*.

Some good critics of my book worried that I was appealing to a selfish motive. Selling out to the ME generation. "Therapeutic forgiving," one called it, turning forgiving from a spiritual act of devotion into a self-help gimmick.

Forgiving to heal your own wounds? Whatever became of forgiving as a simple duty to love our enemy? True forgiving, they claimed, is done only for the sake of the person who wronged us. And then done only because we have a duty to do it. To forgive out of a desire to heal one's own self is ego-centered and selfish. I disagree.

I think forgiving works on both sides of the street. It is a reciprocity. We do ourselves good only when we wish good for the other. And we do the other person good only after we have healed ourselves. Forgiving has to be both ego-centered and other-centered. Otherwise it cannot work.

To clarify my point I am going to make three separate observations.

Serious pain is always egocentric.

Pain screams at us that it is time to pay attention to ourselves. It is an alarm that rings when something is happening to us that needs to be taken care of right away. It asks us to think about ourselves. Getting us to be egocentric is the job pain is supposed to do.

Check out the best-known scream of pain in history—Jesus calling from the cross: "My God, my God, why have you abandoned *me?*" When the pain got most hellish, Jesus focused on what every person in great pain focuses on—his own pain.

The worst pain I ever felt, as far as I can recall, came from a cluster of blood clots that shook loose from my legs and floated up the bloodstream until they docked in my lungs. I bellowed, not against the foul unfairness of life in general, but only against the pain in my own, my very own, and only my very own hurting chest. But you don't have to land in the intensive care unit to discover how egotistical pain is. Ask any woman whose husband has a toothache. Ask anyone close to someone in any horrific pain.

We need to get on top of our own pain before we can get ourselves to do some good to the person who caused it.

Forgiving must heal our pain before it can do any good for the person we forgive.

We prescribe forgiving for two levels of pain: the original pain of being wronged and the reactive pain we call hate or resentment. These two pains blend and, when left unhealed, become one open sore in our wounded memories. Our pain is our hate, and our hate is our pain.

Hate boils down to a yen for another person to feel a proper jolt of serious pain. What sort of pain? It depends on how fierce our hatred is. Perhaps we wish only that good things pass him by. On the other hand we may wish that he never again has a moment's peace. Maybe we call down calamity, hope that his plane will crash, or his new wife will abandon him. Or maybe we hope only that he suffers from remorse for what he did to us. But whatever bad things we want to happen to the person who did bad things to us, we feel it is right for us to want them.

Hate is the most self-righteous of all emotions. We feel deliriously righteous when we hate the evil creature who viciously assaulted us. No one ever feels the pleasure of self-righteousness with such lip-smacking satisfaction as a person chewing on his own hate. This is why we love our hate, coddle it, feed it, stroke it, and above all justify it. But let it settle in for a while, take over the best room in our souls, and it becomes a disagreeable guest who will not leave when our party is over.

So being the kind of pain hate is, it must be healed before we can do anyone else any good at all. It is as simple as that: Forgiving has to heal our pain before it can heal anybody else's pain.

I dare say that God "feels" a lot better for having forgiven us. Certainly he must be enormously delighted that his romance with the human family has a future. The thought of God getting solid benefit out of being a forgiving instead of a vengeful God pleases me enormously.

Wishing the other person well is precisely what we do when we forgive.

When we forgive someone who did us bad, sooner or later we desire good things for the person who did it. This means that we can do ourselves good only by wanting good things for the person who did bad things to us.

My critics say that ideally forgiving should be an act of love. I say that forgiving is nothing at all if it is not an act of love. But it is an act of love that we can do only as we are healed of the wounds we got from the person we loved.

When we forgive someone we give her back the humanity that is ever so worth loving. When we forgive someone we give up on the sweet revenge we had such undeniable right to enjoy. And when we forgive we feel like a person who has just done himself a splendid favor.

Forgiving, like loving, gives us no choice between being self-centered and other-centered. If I love someone only for my sake, my love becomes sick, uncreative, manipulative. If I love someone only for his or her sake, my love becomes fawning charity, demeaning pity. It is the same way with forgiving. We simply have no choice between self-centered forgiving and other-centered forgiving. I can do you good by forgiving you only if I do myself good by forgiving you. It is life's most happy vicious circle.

ॐ

When we forgive we become our own good physician, and the remedy we use percolates from the warm, beating heart of the universe. We are working with the healing energy of the Creator himself. This is why forgiveness does a good thing for the person who wronged us only if it does its first good work inside ourselves.

III

WHOM WE FORGIVE

Ten

WE ONLY FORGIVE
THE ONES WE BLAME

S omething in me does not like to blame people. I always feel better when I get my feet into somebody's shoes, see things from where he stands, and get to understand why he did what he did. He probably just made a mistake, never meant to hurt me at all, and given all I know, he could not help doing what he was doing. When I find out that someone I accused of doing me wrong was not really at fault, it comes as a gentle relief to me. I seem constitutionally tilted toward understanding. A fault? Maybe.

But make no mistake, when I do not blame people, I do not forgive them, either. If we dare not judge, we dare not forgive. We can blame somebody and refuse to forgive him. But we cannot forgive him if we dare not blame him. Blame not, forgive not, and there's the end of it.

I am, I know, swimming against the stream of a popular anti-blame sentiment. A conventional sophistication considers judging other people unenlightened, arrogant, and unwarranted. Needless to say, it is a sentiment that eliminates forgiving from our repertoire of ways to cope with people who do us wrong. I believe the anti-blame people are victims of certain fallacies that are no less fallacious for being attractive to the relativists of our age. I want to run through a few of them and explain why I think they are balderdash.

The "Who Am I to Judge?" Fallacy

This is the perfectionist's fallacy, which holds that imperfect people have no right to blame other imperfect people. If this fallacy were true, nobody should ever blame anybody. But it is not true, and for obvious reasons. If imperfect people don't blame, then the rapists, thieves, and all the other assorted rakes will never be blamed by anyone.

Awareness of our own faultiness should keep us humble when we judge the faults of others, knowing that we may be next to land with our clothes off, belly-up on the examination table. It should also hold us back from jumping into judgment before we know the facts. But if humility were to keep us from judging evil when we see it, then we leave all judgment to fools.

I am aware that Jesus, when faced with the woman caught in adultery, said to her accusers, in effect: "Let [only] him that is without sin cast the first stone." He did not mean that it was okay for sinners to cast the second stone after the righteous got in the first shot. Sinners should not throw any stones at all. But we need to recall that stoning people, in his day, was tantamount to assigning them to hell. So it is reasonable to suppose that he meant only that it was not a sinner's prerogative to bury any fellow sinner under a pile of stones and thus consign him to the pit of fire.

When we blame wrongdoers for doing wrong, we are only holding them accountable on earth for one piece of bad action. We do not mean to assign them to perdition. We just hold them accountable for what they did between noon and three on Friday past.

We make a big mistake if we disqualify ourselves from doing this much. The moment we say, "Who am I to judge?" we resign our membership in the family of rational human beings. And we are reneging on one of the most important tasks assigned to rational human beings: to size up people's actions the best we can and to assign responsibility for them. Which is to say that imperfect people have not only the right but an obligation to blame people.

The Blame-Share Fallacy

According to the blame-share fallacy, anyone who shares responsibility for what went wrong forfeits her right to blame the person who did it. The fallacy assumes that if we bear some responsibility for the poverty in which the thief grew up, we are as guilty as he is for mugging us. In this vein, the Allies who crushed Germany after World War I had no right to blame Hitler for starting World War II. The truth, in my opinion, is that we must blame people who do wrong even if we helped make the wrong possible.

It is true that none of us is an island unto ourselves, even in the doing of bad things to other people. We are all—more or less and for good or ill—nudged into the path we finally travel. A codependent wife who made it easy for her husband to drink may still blame him if he slugs her when he has had a few. A woman who dressed provocatively may still blame a man for raping her. A lenient father who did not dare to discipline may still blame a son for beating on his mother. All this goes without saying.

The notion of coresponsibility is not a fallacy. But the notion that we cannot hold people accountable unless they alone are totally responsible *is* a fallacy. And it is a fallacy to say that if we helped make it possible for them to do wrong, we should not blame them when they do wrong. People who are coresponsible should temper their blame of others with blame for themselves. But humble blaming is still blaming. And humble blaming leads to humble forgiving. Which is the only good kind.

The "To Understand All Is to Forgive All" Fallacy

According to this fallacy, understanding is equivalent to forgiving. If we can slip into the shoes of the person who hurt us, we may realize that he could not have helped himself. His father beat him. His mother kept him at her apron strings and never let him grow up. His therapist encouraged him to act on his feelings. If you really understood him, you would be able to see him for what he is—a victim who needs love and not blame, excusing and not forgiving.

Listen to author Fay Weldon grumble (in her book, *Female Friends)* about her mother: "Understand, and forgive, my mother said, and the effort has quite exhausted me. . . . Preach acceptance to wives and tolerance to husbands. . . . Understand, forgive, accept. . . . O Mother, what you taught me! And what a miserable, crawling, sniveling way to go. . . ." Your mother had it all wrong, Fay Weldon.

If we understand why someone did what he did, we do not forgive him. We forgive him only when we *cannot* understand why he did it. If we really understood why someone had to hurt us, we would know he could not help himself, and we would excuse him instead of blame him. And if we excuse someone, we do not need to forgive him because we only forgive the ones we blame.

It's like this:

When we understand why he had to do it, we excuse him.

When we excuse him, we do not blame him.

WE ONLY FORGIVE THE ONES WE BLAME

When we do not blame him, we do not forgive him.

The Fatalist Fallacy

This is the fallacy which holds that people who wrong us are not to be blamed because they are only acting out a script written for them by their genes. Or by their environment. Or by God. Or by a combination of the three. We are naive, fatalists tell us, if we think that people are responsible when in fact they are programmed.

If we observe that people really do feel responsible, the fatalist answers that their feelings are also part of their fate. If we insist on treating people as responsible human beings, the fatalist says it is because we are fated to make simplistic moral judgments. Nobody wins an argument with a fatalist.

Blaming people for doing whatever bad things they do does not mean we think everyone is *totally* responsible for everything they do. Nor does it mean that we think all people are *equally* responsible. Whatever evil influences were buzzing around them or inside them when they did the bad things, they still had the power not to do them. Therefore we blame them. And only then, if we are so inclined, do we forgive them.

We do not have to reject the link between our inlaid genetic maps and our current decisions. We do not have to reject the providence of a God who oversees all our destinies. All we need to do is hold on to a belief that, in spite of all the influences on us, we do have power to act on our own initiative, we do not have to do what we do, and to that extent we are accountable for what we do.

We should remember that blaming a person who wronged us is one of the better compliments we can ever pay her. You don't reproach a tomcat for prowling. Or a sleek leopard for jumping a gentle gazelle. Tomcats and leopards are blameless.

The honor of being blamed and forgiven is reserved for the children of God.

Of course, the honor does not belong to everybody we get it into our heads to blame. The fact that it is right for one person to blame another in a given situation tempts us to suppose that we must be right *whenever* we blame someone. But this, too, is a temptation that we are free to reject.

This gets us to my final question. How do we know who is to be blamed for bad things that happen?

Is everyone who belongs to a group or a gang that injures someone responsible for what the group or gang does? Does everybody in Germany need to be forgiven for what the butchers of Auschwitz did? Everybody? Even the children? Does someone who suffered at the hands of the Nazis in 1945 have a right to forgive or refuse to forgive Germans who were boys and girls in 1945? Perhaps to declare them unforgivable?

Allow Joseph Polak to answer the question.

Joseph Polak was three years old in 1945 when the guards of the concentration camp at Bergen-Belsen loaded him and his family into a packed freight car. They stacked 2,500 people on that freight train and gave them no food to eat or water to drink. The camp was not far off and most of them could survive that long. But the engineer missed his switch, got confused, lost his way, and his train ground blindly eastward, on and on for several days. Finally it came to a halt at a tiny village in eastern Germany called Troebetz. Five hundred people died horrible deaths on the lost death train before it stopped, and many more died soon after.

Joseph Polak survived, is now a distinguished rabbi in Boston, and told his story in the September 1995 issue of *Commonweal*. In 1995, to mark the fiftieth anniversary of that horrendous ride, Rabbi Polak and some other survivors took a train along the same route that the death train took from Belsen to Troebetz. Before they left Belsen, the officials of the town held a service for them. The minister of culture spoke. In his speech he reminded the survivors that 85 percent of the present population of Germany were only five years old or less when the horror happened—his point being, of course, that these children—now adults—should not be held responsible for the killer freight train.

Rabbi Polak rejected the cultural minister's plea out of hand. As Polak listened to him, he silently spoke these terrible words to the adult Germans of 1995 who had been fated to be the German children of 1945.

"The deeds of your parents cannot be forgotten, and as long as memory stirs . . . you are doomed to be their representatives, and your hands will be stained with blood that you yourselves may not have spilled. For as long as people remember history, or hear a Jewish story, or see a Jewish child, you are destined to take responsibility for this darkness and never, ever to be forgiven for it."

Never, ever to be forgiven? Are all Germans who were little children when the Holocaust happened forever under a curse? And their children after them? By the same law, would all generations of Jews be cursed for their fathers' genocide of the ancient Canaanites? And all American children cursed forever because their fathers made slaves of black people? When does judgment cease? If we curse all children for the evil their parents do, do we not doom most of the human race?

I have profound respect for the rabbi's moral passion. I, too, believe that individuals in certain tragic senses share the destiny of the whole people. But I do not concede to Rabbi Polak the right to condemn all the children of guilty Germans to be unforgiven forever. The little children of Germany did not send a single Jew or Christian to a concentration camp. Three-year-old boys and girls did not stash the Polak family into that death train. The rabbi would have no right to forgive these people even if his heart nudged him to do so. By the same token, he has no right to declare them unforgivable.

We need, then, to answer one final question before we stop talking about blaming. How do we know when someone is to blame for the injuries we suffered? I suggest three tests.

He did it.

As a simple matter of fact, he did it. You know he did it, and he knows he did it. Maybe he admitted it; maybe somebody saw him do it; maybe you were right there taking it on the chin when he did it. However you came to know it, you are sure it was he who did it. If you don't know, hold the forgiving.

He meant to do it.

He knew what he was doing; he intended to do it. He was neither predestined nor fated to do it. He was not drugged. He was not the victim of a mishap or accident. He may not have intended that what he did should hurt you as much as it did. But he did intend to do it. And this is why he is either a target for revenge or a candidate for forgiving.

He initiated the action.

Nobody forced him. Sure, his dad was a drunk; his uncle is a drunk, and look at his brothers—all drunks. It's in the genes, bred in the bone. But it was he who got the notion in his head to drive somewhere. It was he who turned the ignition key and put his foot on the pedal. And it was he who drove in the path of a car headed his way and rammed a

WE ONLY FORGIVE THE ONES WE BLAME

carload of innocents. He began it, did it, and finished it. So you blame him.

In sum, if he did it, intended to do it, and initiated the action, he is accountable for doing it. If what he did wounded and wronged you personally, you blame him. Only then do you consider forgiving him. You must remember that you might be wrong. It is always possible that he might be wholly innocent. So let no one rush to blame. My point is only that forgiving always comes with blame attached.

∾

Forgiving is for the tough-minded. It is not for the soft-headed who cannot abide people who make judgments on other people's actions. If we dare not blame, we dare not forgive. Forgiving is for people who know their own faults but who recognize a wrong and dare to name it when they feel it done to them and have the wisdom and grace to forgive it.

Eleven

FORGIVING PEOPLE WHO DO NOT SAY THEY ARE SORRY

Before day had dawned one January morning in 1984, Pope John Paul walked down a dark hall in Rebibbia prison in the city of Rome to visit a prisoner named Mehmet Ali Agca. Ali Agca was the terrorist who had, a few weeks earlier, waited in the shadowy nooks of the Vatican until the holy father appeared, maneuvered himself to the front of the crowd, aimed a pistol at him, and shot him in the chest. The pope recovered. And now he stood in front of the cell, shook the hand of the man who fired a bullet at his heart, and said: "I forgive you."

The media of the world made quite a fuss over the pope's unexpected mercy. Skeptics said that he was only doing his job; he is a professional forgiver; it's all in a day's work for him. Cynics guessed he was doing it for the cameras, a media event arranged for the evening news by the Vatican press secretary. But most of us needed to believe that the pope was acting as a generous human being who simply wanted to forgive a man who had done him serious wrong.

For believers, it was not the pope's sincerity that was in doubt, but his wisdom. Ali Agca had not given a single hint that he was sorry for what he did. He certainly had not asked the pope to forgive him. It's even possible that he had a good

87

laugh about it as soon as the pope left, and if he had had a gun, he would have shot the pope again, then and there, while he heard those words of forgiveness. So what was the point of the pope's forgiveness?

Was this acclaimed display of unwanted mercy a misguided and dangerous example for a pope to set? For a spiritual leader to encourage battered people to forgive the persons who battered them once and may be getting set to assault them again? Does it send the wrong message to the bad and the mean of the world? Does it suggest that if they can shoot popes and get forgiven, maybe they can get away with anything?

To bring the case against forgiving unrepentant wrongdoers down from high church drama to a more ordinary person's pains, I will turn from the holy father to an unholy husband named Conrad Coars, known among his colleagues at Badnose College in Waterloo, Iowa, of course, as Concoars.

Concoars was smitten by Ogvla Grymjek on his first visit to a Pentecostal bookstore in Slovakia where he was spending a sabbatical looking into whether the Slovaks might use Iowa hybrid corn seed to get a new start in free enterprise agriculture. Ogvla's family, Gypsy not far back, had thrown her out at the time she converted to the Pentecostal faith, and she was all too ready to have her dreams come true when Concoars talked of taking her back to America with him. They were married in Bratislava and were off to Iowa as soon as a visa came.

Back in Waterloo, Concoars took Ogvla's "Americanization" into his own hands; he turned her into his child, to have and to humiliate as the mood hit him. Teaching her the language and the amenities was only one channel for humiliating her in mean and crazy ways. For instance, he had his own method for teaching her the proper thing to say to older colleagues at faculty socials.

"When I introduce you to an older lady," he would tell her, "always bow slightly and say very slowly: 'I am extremely stupid.' " Concoars invited curious friends to dinner before Ogvla had learned to cook American food in an American kitchen, and when the meal began he would say things like: "Of course, my little Ogvla, when she gets behind a stove, thinks she is still in Bratislava making stinking cabbage soup for the Holy Rollers."

Ogvla's pain increased with her increasing consciousness of what was being done to her. She enrolled at Badnose where faculty families could study without paying tuition and began with a course called "English for Non-English-Speaking People." That done, she was on her way to a degree. Halfway into the program, however, she took a detour of sorts, a job off campus as something like a clerical assistant at a law office. Then something really bad happened.

Concoars was fired for offering women students the opportunity to trade sexual favors for good grades. He had been censured before for harassing female staff persons. Ogvla knew about this, and she had heard, too, that someone had seen him getting close to a woman student in the parking lot. Until now, she was afraid to say anything to him. But when the Waterloo sky fell on Concoars, she just packed some clothes and walked away, alone, with nowhere to go but back to her Pentecostal refuge. The well-meaning minister asked her to consider forgiving Concoars. "Forgive him," he said, "or you may never be happy again."

"I shall neevair forgave him, neevair, neevair," she told her minister. "He stealed me from my country and he made me shamed of self, no I shall neevair forgeeve him."

In a few years, Ogvla rose above the herd of filing clerks to become a legal secretary. But inside her own spirit she sank into a black pool of shame and rage, afraid now to trust any male hand stretched out to her.

Then Concoars came back. He had located Ogvla, followed her for a few days, and then came knocking. "After all I did for you, it seems to me that you owe it to me to forgive me and let bygones be bygones," he whined. "I took you out of your misery, didn't I? If it were not for me you would still be back there with nobody but your Slovak Holy Rollers for family. Sure I made mistakes, but you've done all right for yourself anyway, seems to me, so why not forgive and forget and start over?"

Now the Pentecostal minister, the only man she trusted, made a second appraisal of Ogvla's situation. "No. You mustn't forgive him. Not now, not until he repents. Nobody should get forgiven until he says he is sorry." Which left Ogvla where she was—alone, enraged, wounded, shamed, and with no chance for healing until Concoars had a change of heart.

Did the minister make sense? Would Ogvla have been a dupe if she had forgiven a brute too mired in self-deception to see the meanness of the wrong he had done to her? Would it have made sense for Ogvla to forgive Concoars even though chances were that, if she let him back, he would have gone back to his old ways as surely as an addict goes back to his dope?

There are strong arguments against forgiving an un-repentant enemy, and I respect them even though I am not persuaded by them. There are, as I count them, five plausible reasons not to forgive people who do not say they are sorry. I am going to report them one by one and give my answer to each one in turn.

If a person who wrongs us does not repent, he doesn't deserve to be forgiven.

Of course, he does not *deserve* to be forgiven. Nobody does. And all the tears in Neptune's ocean do not earn him the right or make him deserving. Forgiving under any circumstance is only for people who don't deserve it. Being sorry for the wrong we did does not earn us a right to be forgiven. How could it? There is no such thing as a right to be forgiven. Forgiving flows always and only from what theologians call grace—unearned, undeserved favor. Grace that is earned is not grace at all. In an odd way, if we deserved to be forgiven, we would not need to be.

Forgiving someone who does not repent is just too hard to do.

If someone comes on his knees, eyes red from weeping, heart in hand, groaning to all that he is the lowest of louses, and running over with promises never to do it again, it is easier to forgive him than if he struts in like a peacock. Forgiving the hardheaded, dry-eyed unrepentant is hard indeed. And yet, when we realize that forgiving is the only remedy for the pain the offender left us with, the only way to heal the hurt he caused, we have an incentive to forgive no matter if his heart is hard as flint. In short, forgiving unrepentant people is a no-lose opportunity—difficult to do but with a harvest of healing.

To forgive an unrepentant person is not fair to ourselves.

Yes, we must be fair to ourselves. But are we fair to ourselves when we prolong a bitterness that is shriveling our spirits? Are we fair to ourselves if we let our abuser or betrayer or deceiver decide for us when we may be healed of the pain he caused? I plead the victim's right to heal herself, and if forgiving someone who never says he is sorry is the way to do it, she is unfair to herself if she declines.

To forgive an unrepentant person is dangerous; if he feels no sorrow for what he did, he is likely to do it again.

The fear that forgiveness will encourage the culprit to repeat his wrong is rooted in a misunderstanding of forgiveness. Forgiving is not tolerance. Forgivers are not sentimental fools. Nor does forgiving a person mean that we invite him to get close enough to hurt us again. When we forgive someone who is not sorry for what he has done, we do not forget, and we do not intend to let it happen again.

The Bible says that we have to repent before we can get forgiven.

The apostle Peter had just finished his keynote speech at the birth of the Christian church. People asked him: "What should we do?" And Peter told them: "Repent, and be baptized . . . so that your sins may be forgiven" (Acts 2:38 NRSV). It is clear that, when we are dealing with God, we have no right to expect forgiveness unless we ask for it in sorrow. But does this mean that we should not forgive anyone unless he is sorry for what he did?

I think not. Let me offer two reasons why I do not think the apostle was saying that we should forgive only after the person who hurts us repents for what he did.

First, we are dealing in this biblical passage with people who want to *be* forgiven. We are not dealing with people who need to *do* the forgiving. The question is whether anyone has a right to expect to be forgiven if he does not repent. The plain and simple answer is no: A person who wrongs God should not *expect* God to forgive her unless she is sorry for the wrong she did. So much for that.

Second, when people want to be forgiven by God, they want to be reunited with him at the same time. But God wants reunion with integrity. And repentance is nothing but simple honesty about what we did to break our connection with God. This is why a person cannot *expect* to be forgiven by God unless he first repents.

The same goes for us mortals. Nobody can expect to be forgiven and reunited with the person he wounded unless he repents of what he did to hurt her in the first place. No one should ever presume on our forgiving and certainly not on our willingness to restore a relationship that he destroyed. But when we are the ones who have been hurt, we simply cannot afford to wait for the other person to come to his senses before we begin healing ourselves.

So far I have been answering the arguments *against* forgiving people who do not say they are sorry. Now I want to offer a single clear and positive reason *for* doing it. It comes down to something as plain as potatoes: The person who hurt us should not be the person who decides whether or when we should recover from the pain he brought us. We should not be kept from healing by the muleheadedness of a heel who wounded and wronged us and will not even own up to it.

I am going to sum up by offering six good reasons for forgiving people who wounded us even though they do not seem to care—six reasons to forgive people who never say they are sorry:

> Forgiving is something good we do for ourselves; we should not have to wait for permission from the person who did something bad to us.
>
> When we forgive someone who does not say he's sorry, we are not issuing him a welcome back to the relationship we had before; if he wants to come back he must come in sorrow.
>
> To *give* forgiveness requires nothing but a desire to be free of our resentment. To *receive* forgiveness requires

sorrow for what we did to give someone reason to be resentful.

We cannot *expect* to be forgiven without sorrow for the wrong we did. We should not *demand* sorrow for the wrong someone did to us.

Repentance does not earn the right to forgiveness; it only prepares us to receive the gift.

A wounded person should not put her future happiness in the hands of the person who made her miserable.

∿

When the pope forgave Ali Agca, the man who shot him, he was only untying the knot in his own heart. The pope may never know for sure whether Ali Agca ever received his forgiveness. What he does know is that there is no hatred in his heart that keeps love out of Ali Agca's heart.

And what of Ogvla Grymjek? If she followed her minister's advice and is waiting for Concoars to repent, she is surrendering her right to her own healing to the very clod who caused her such pain. If she forgave Concoars for the pain-riddled shame he caused her, she gave herself freedom to walk without him toward a distant happiness she never had with him.

The rule is the same for a pope who has been shot or anyone else who has been violated. It is folly to let the person who wounded us decide whether we should forgive him for having done it.

Twelve

FORGIVING OURSELVES

Forgiving ourselves is a tough nut to crack. Which is probably a good thing. Forgiving ourselves *should* be hard. Possible, yes, easy, no. If forgiving ourselves comes easy, chances are, we are only excusing ourselves, ducking blame, and not really forgiving ourselves at all.

When it comes to forgiving ourselves, we run right into four problems that need solving. First, there is a logistics problem: If we forgive ourselves, who is forgiving whom? Forgiving takes two—someone who forgives and someone who gets forgiven. So it is reasonable to ask whether solitaire forgiving even makes sense. Second, there is a moral problem: What right do I have to hurt someone else and then conveniently forgive myself for doing him wrong? Then there are two practical problems. What do we forgive ourselves for? And how do we go about doing it? I suggest we take on these four problems, one at a time.

Does it make sense to forgive ourselves?

Forgiveness usually takes a cast of two. Solitaire forgiving, some people say, makes no more sense than solo tennis.

But what makes forgiving ourselves seem odd is really the

95

remarkable oddness of the human self. Our power to transcend ourselves is unique in the world of creatures. One of me can step alongside the other me and take stock of what I see while the other me feels either judged or loved by me. We constantly play the role of both the actor and the acted upon. We lie to ourselves. We congratulate ourselves. We enjoy ourselves. We blame ourselves. Why should we not forgive ourselves?

We feel a need to forgive ourselves because the part of us that gets blamed feels split off from the part that does the blaming. One self feels despised and rejected by the other. We are exiled from our own selves, which is no way to live. This is why we need to forgive ourselves and why it makes sense to do it: We are ripped apart inside, and forgiving ourselves is the only way we heal the split.

Who gives us the right to forgive ourselves?

Remember that only victims have a right to forgive. But when we forgive ourselves it is the culprit who forgives.

If a drunk driver ran over one of my grandchildren and told me a few days later that he had forgiven himself for what he did, I think I would wring his neck. Does a murderer have the right to forgive himself for cutting somebody's throat and then expect congratulations for his triumph of grace?

Let's face it: Forgiving ourselves is a questionable operation. We are all too prone to excuse ourselves anyway, and forgiving ourselves could be a cheap trick to avoid responsibility. Forgive other people who hurt you, if you wish, forgive them anything and everything they ever did to you, but be sure you have the right to forgive yourself for what you do to them. People cannot just go around forgiving themselves for anything and everything they do to other people. Do-it-yourself absolution requires some sort of validation.

Who validates our self-forgiving? It seems to me that only

two persons are authorized to issue us a self-forgiveness license. One of them is the person we wronged. The other is the God who feels sorrow when we wound his children.

When a person asks us to forgive him, he is also asking permission to forgive himself. What he wants is more than freedom from our judgment. He wants freedom from *his own*. In one sense, we are the only ones on earth who can set him free to free himself.

We must pay for the license to forgive ourselves. We pay in the currency of remorse. Just as none but the contrite has a right to expect forgiveness from others, none but the contrite has a right to forgive himself. Remorse is a price we pay to forgive ourselves. For when we forgive ourselves we are the forgiven as well as the forgiver.

But let us say you feel remorse. You would give all you own if you could undo what you did to someone you love. And you have gone on your knees, empty-handed, begging pardon from the person you injured. She knows true grovel when she sees it. But still she looks into your beseeching eyes and tells you to pour your tears down the toilet.

What now? Are you sentenced to the lonely hell of your self-condemnation because your unforgiving victim chooses to choke on her own hate?

No, there is Another. It is, I believe, the calling of God to suffer. Max De Pree, who wrote the deservedly acclaimed book *Leadership Is an Art,* says that it is the job of a chief executive officer not to cause suffering but to bear it. God fits the same picture; being God is a painful occupation. And he never suffers more than when we harm his children. Why do we seek forgiveness from God when it is a human being we have wronged? It is not because we know in our hearts that when we have done it to one of his children we have done it to him? This is why he can forgive us for his pain even though the human person we hurt will not forgive us.

But having a right to forgive ourselves does not give us the ability to do it anymore than my right to visit a state park provides me with a car to get there.

The first thing we need to know when we try to forgive ourselves is what it is that we are forgiving ourselves for. So before we talk about the how, we need to ask about the what.

What do we forgive ourselves for?

We forgive ourselves for what we did, not for what we are.

Doing wrong, not being wrong, is what we can forgive ourselves for. We don't forgive ourselves for being bad sorts of persons. Not for being failures. Not for being stupid. Or ugly. Not even for being bad. If we try to forgive ourselves for being the sorts of persons we are, we may get forgiving ourselves confused with accepting ourselves. Relief from self-judgment comes by forgiving grace. Relief from self-rejection comes by accepting grace. So a simple rule to remember is this: We forgive ourselves for what we do; we accept ourselves as we are, sometimes in spite of who we are, sometimes because of who we are, but always *as* we are.

We forgive ourselves for specific things we did.

Forgiving ourselves for a mess of things in general is like trying to kill a flock of geese with a baseball bat. Sooner or later we have to get down to individual cases. We can be wracked by shame for being a wholesale failure. But we have to forgive ourselves piecemeal. Nail it down. Put it in verbs. What did you actually do? When did you do it? Where did it happen? Be concrete. Shake off glob guilt. Keep a focus on the particular.

We forgive ourselves for wrongful things that we deserve blame for doing.

A lot of people worry about forgiving themselves when all they really need is a sense of proportion. You don't need to forgive yourself for not living up to your mother's expectations. Nor for failing to match the fantasy your husband thought he was marrying. And you do not need to be forgiven for violating religious traditions that have nothing to do with right or wrong. Nor for failing to be the hero you feel you ought to have been.

Carl Tuyl remembers a moment in his own history when he didn't measure up to the hero he so terribly wanted to be. And today he wonders whether he can forgive himself for being a coward once, more than half a century ago. Actually, Carl is a courageous man. I know of one time he risked his neck to rescue a man trapped under the ice of a frozen lake and came within an inch of drowning himself. Still he looks back with unforgiven guilt at one flitting instant during the war when he did not leap to heroic distinction. He was nothing but a boy, mind you, seventeen years old, but already in the underground resistance, too young to be a man but not too young to expect himself to be.

It happened when he and a small group from the underground were rounded up by the Gestapo and loaded onto the bed of a rickety truck for transport to the concentration camp. He was sitting next to the rear gate of the truck with an older friend, a man who had been hiding out in Carl's house. Lumbering down a rough country road, the truck had to slow down for potholes once in a while. His friend whispered, "When I give the signal, jump."

At the next pothole, his friend jumped, got away, and made it back to his group. Carl froze. He couldn't jump, didn't dare. He landed in the concentration camp, somehow survived, and now, more than a half century later, sighs: "Coming face to face with your own weakness is no pleasant thing. The moment of my cowardice lives on in me, and still today I cannot forgive myself. . . ."

Ah, Carl, you and I are brothers under the skin. My ancient bits and pieces of childhood cowardice haunt and shame me, too. I cannot forget that moment when, as a boy of sixteen, working behind the counter at an ice cream shop, I kept my mouth shut when the waitresses refused to wait on a black couple. I did not dare. Not a pleasant thing to think about. But a boyhood failure to rise to the heroic is not something for an old man to worry about forgiving himself for.

We forgive ourselves for what we blame ourselves for.

We can forgive ourselves only for things we hold ourselves responsible for. Blame and forgiving are matched components. A person without the courage to blame himself is like a paramedic who has an unlisted phone number. If our conscience can't reach us, we won't be bothered.

We would rather explain ourselves than blame ourselves. If we can explain ourselves, we can excuse ourselves. And most people who ask others to forgive them are really asking to be excused. But when I admit that I did it, that I did not have to do it, that what I did was wrong, and that I wish to God I had not done it, when I admit this, I blame myself. And I am ready to forgive myself.

We forgive ourselves for what we feel forgiven for.

If I do blame myself for wronging someone, I will still not feel free to forgive myself unless I feel forgiven by the other person. When I am forgiven, I accept the gift of her forgiveness as a license to forgive myself. When I digest her grace inside myself, her permission becomes my power.

But what can a person do if she blames herself, asks to be forgiven, and has the door of rejection slammed in her face? Her only option is an appeal to God. She can admit her guilt to God and seek from him what she could not find in the other. When he forgives her, and she ingests his grace, actually feels forgiven in her guts, she has both the permission and the power to forgive herself even if the person she wounded does not forgive her.

The feeling of being forgiven and the feeling of forgiving ourselves are so much alike that there is no point in trying to keep them distinct. In fact, the line between feeling forgiven and forgiving ourselves is so thin that we can seldom tell for sure when we have crossed it. When we are bone-tired of the guilt, and we have asked to be forgiven, maybe then the word will get to us, get inside us: You are forgiven. You are *forgiven*. You *are* forgiven. And when it finally sinks in, we are qualified and we are enabled to forgive ourselves.

Now for some tips. We often make forgiving ourselves even harder than it need be. Let me make a few suggestions.

How can we go about forgiving ourselves?

We tell it to ourselves.

There is a well-tested power in pronouncement. The Catholic church knew what it was doing when it gave priests the authority to pronounce absolution as if it were a done deal every time. We need to give ourselves absolution. And we need to pronounce it to ourselves.

Say it out loud. Say it straight into the eyes of the reflection you see in a mirror: "God forgives you and so do I." You may feel like a clown. But do it anyway. If you dare to say it, you have already begun to do it. It is a creative hypocrisy—pretending to do what you really do intend to do—that becomes real even while you pretend.

We repeat it.

Self-forgiveness is not self-induced amnesia. When the memory of the horrid thing we did clicks on, the toxin of guilt spills through and condemns us again. So we need to stand before the mirror, and say it again. Forgiving is seldom done once and for all. It almost always needs repeating. So say it a hundred times if you need to, say it until the meaning begins to filter through your left brain into your soul. Once you get the hang of it, the repeats will get easier and the relief will get faster.

We keep it to ourselves.

There is no law that says you have to tell other people that you have forgiven yourself. And you probably won't say it well, which will make things even worse. The person you have wounded and who will not forgive you may feel doubly resentful of you if you seem to flaunt the freedom God gave you to forgive yourself. She may spit on your peace. Better, all things considered, to keep it to yourself.

We act like it even if we don't talk about it.

Our unforgiving victims may not want us to act like forgiven people. They may be miffed unless we crawl into our holes like groundhogs who have seen their shadows. Our unforgiving victims won't want us at their friends' parties. They will bristle when we traipse to the same Communion rail as they do. They may want us frozen in self-judgment forever.

But never mind, we have a license. If God gave us permission to forgive ourselves we should walk into all the old places where we felt at home before our fall. Doing it will give us the courage to keep on forgiving ourselves.

We do something extravagant.

Recall again the woman who crashed a dinner party where Jesus was a guest. The host, a man of parts in his religious community, did not want her there. But she sneaked in anyway, plunked herself on the floor where Jesus was sitting, took off his sandals, and washed his feet with expensive oils.

What a gamble! She was liable to be dragged out bodily and tossed into the street. What made her do something that crazy? Jesus understood why she did it. She had been forgiven much. And anybody who knows she has been forgiven much loves much. This was why she felt so free. And then, once she had done it, she went away more sure than ever that she had really been forgiven.

If you want to feel like a person who has forgiven herself, do the sorts of impulsive things that forgiven people might be inclined to do. Send roses to the woman who will not forgive you. She may give them to the cleaning lady—what do you care? Write a letter to an old friend you have not been in touch with for years. Give a couple of twenties to a homeless person. Do anything nice that the practical part of you will tell you is nutty. Celebrate the miracle you are performing on yourself by creating a little miracle for somebody else.

There you have them, five ways to make sure you are forgiving yourself for the right things and five suggestions for actually doing it when you need to. Try them. When you give it an honest try, you will be on your way. Remember, though, that you will never be awfully good at it. We will always be mucking our way through grace.

Thirteen

FORGIVING GOD

Anybody who knows God at all knows that forgiving God makes no sense and is actually an outrageous idea. Forgiving always has blame in its lining, and God never does anything he can be blamed for. Or even to apologize for. Forgiving God would be tantamount to impeaching him; a God who needs to be forgiven for doing bad things to people does not deserve to be God.

Yet I have known decent people who were assaulted by sorrow so heavy and pains so unfair that they have had cause to wonder. How could God sit in heaven serenely surrounded by his seraphim and cherubim and watch while three of his earthly children were slaughtered in one cruel moment by a drunken driver? God could have saved them with his little pinkie. But he didn't lift a finger. The Holy One had some explaining to do.

I have, I suppose, as much awe for the maker of the universe as most people do, but I do not believe that he would take it personally if my suffering friends got it into their heads to forgive him. Forgiving God, like getting married, is certainly not something to be done lightly, if at all, and it certainly never hurts to think about it before jumping in.

I have wondered sometimes *whether it might ever make sense* to forgive God. To get an answer, I consulted two sources of simple common sense—divine and human—about how God carries on when people are wronged and what we should do about him when things go badly wrong with us.

First then, the voice of divine common sense.

I imagined once that before I was born here I had lived forever, it seemed, as a happy angel in heaven. God called me into his presence one day to make me a proposition. I could, if I chose, go on floating for endless years on cushions of air and never stub my toe—let alone catch a head cold or get cancer—running God's errands. But he thought I might want to consider a change.

"What I offer you is an opportunity to take up a new existence as a humanoid on our little planet Earth. I would nestle you into a fragile organism called a body, in which you would work and play and love with other embodied creatures like yourself."

"Sounds interesting," I said. "What would be the advantages for me?" (I was a cheeky angel.)

"Several. But just to mention a few, you could get hugs from people, and I think you might like that. You could eat chicken salad, take pictures of sunsets, and hear lovely symphonies on compact discs. Maybe the best part is that you could make love to another humanoid and have a family."

"Sounds good. What's the downside?"

"The downside is that being a body makes you vulnerable to pain. Bodies break down now and then, which is troublesome. When you bump into the hard things you find on earth, you will tend to bruise badly. And the fun you'll have loving people with bodies invites a lot of mischief that you won't really understand until you try it. In any case, you cannot have the pleasures of body-life without the risk of pain."

"Well, as long as the odds are reasonable."

"There is one more risk, the chanciest part of the adventure. It is the freedom that comes with being human. Freedom will be what you need most, but if you misuse it, you can lose it. And that can cause deep trouble."

"Well, at least I know what I will be in for."

"No, you don't. Not yet. But I will promise you one thing: Whatever happens, I'll be on call. What do you say to my proposition?"

I did not think about it twice. The idea of being human struck me as the chance of a lifetime. "Yes, I'll go."

I never seriously regretted the move. But I took some lumps from being human. Sometimes I felt as if God had gone on a leave of absence and left an incompetent lieutenant in charge of the shop. And when I faulted him for it, he came back with this unwelcome common sense.

"Your complaints have reached me," God said. "What is it? Do you want to go back to being an angel again?"

"No, sir, body-life suits me just fine. I want to stay here as long as I can."

"Then why the whimpers? You were only too glad to accept the conditions for being human. You know you cannot have body-life without the risk of pain any more than you can have sun without shadows. Common sense, my son."

I felt like a rather complete ninny for blaming God when his common sense reminded me that pain comes with being a body the way skin comes with being a tomato.

Then my heart spoke. *I know that some pain is the price of being human, but surely the price gets too high sometimes. A woman's husband and her three children get wiped out in a flash by a drunk driver. A child is raped by her father. And, in the shadows of memory, never going away, the Holocaust. Are horrors like these really part of the deal?*

As my heart complained, God came back with some more, this time severe, common sense.

"Who are you to blame me?"

"Well, I'm your child, for one thing, and it just seems to me that some people suffer more pain than being human on a broken planet calls for. And when they do, you don't seem to respond. It seems to me that we have a right to expect a little more attention from you when bad things get out of control."

"Hold it right there, son. Put your hand over your mouth. Can a moth tell an eagle how to fly? Can a mole measure the Milky Way? I am the Wholly Other One. I invented the world. How dare you tell me how to run it?"

The Wholly Other had me.

"I am a fool," I said. "You'll get no more complaints from me."

So I kept silence before him. And I went even further. I began thinking positive thoughts about unfair pain. Since God is good and can do no ill, and since he allows his children to suffer a lot of horrible pain, it must be that pain is good for us—somehow. Otherwise, he would not let it happen.

Mind you, I am talking about serious pain, the kind of pain good people suffer at the hands of bad people, pain that has no purpose and makes no sense. I am talking about the very kind of unfair wounds that we are told to forgive our fellow human beings for. Maybe, if we see it in the right light, even the worst kind of pain will turn out to be a blessing in disguise—God's gift. Not something to forgive him for but to thank him for instead.

Having been put in my place by God, I looked for some human common sense on the matter. For instance, think of pain as God's way of getting us to listen to him. We get so distracted by our hot pursuit of security and pleasure that we forget to keep tuned in to God. We practically force him to use pain as a way of shouting to get our attention. I recall C. S. Lewis saying (in *The Problem of Pain*) that pain is God's megaphone to rouse a deaf world. He uses it to shake us up and make us listen.

This positive thought would be more convincing if I always knew what God was shouting through the megaphone. He may be telling me something, but I am not at all sure *what*. Besides, it sometimes seems that God is the one who is not paying attention. My pain is *my* megaphone to get through to *him*. The megaphone metaphor cuts two ways with me.

Another positive thought is that pain is God's hammer. He uses it to hammer out character. God is a sculptor, shaping us into the better persons he intends us to be, and we do not provide him with easy raw material. So when our pain gets unusually severe, we can be sure that it is God working on us, chisel in one hand, hammer in the other, chipping off our hardened vices, sculpting out the better person we were meant to be, and giving our patience some exercise in the bargain.

We get to be better persons for having felt the bad pain. If we have our values in order, we will recognize the benefit in pain. Sometimes. Other times, the pain is so big and the improvement in character so small that it is hard to see the benefit. Someone told Nicholas Wolterstorff (who tells us about it in his incomparably beautiful book *Lament for a Son*) that his son Eric fell off a mountain ledge and died because God had shaken the mountain. A woman once told me that she believed her little girl was killed by a truck because God had taken over the wheel. Why would God shake a mountain or take over the steering wheel so that someone's child would die? Does God take the life of a child to improve a parent's character?

The thought is grotesque to me. It strikes me that what we say in defense of God is, in this case, an insult. I know that many gentle and wise people believe God *always* has a good purpose for allowing unfair pain to happen to us. And I know that my personal revulsion against this idea does not prove that these people are wrong. It only means that I cannot stomach it; my deepest sense of who and what God is will not let me.

My third positive thought was that pain is to our lives what a bold, dark stroke is to a beautiful painting. The world is to be God's masterpiece. A luminous portrait that reflects the great Artist's glory. Once we look at the whole of it, we will see that the dark shadows make the painting more beautiful than it could have been without them. The worst of our pain shows off the best of God's world, and the two of them together make up the best possible world.

To all this I pose just one simple question: Will the abuse of one innocent child ever make God's creation a more beautiful place? My heart says NEVER.

I find myself recoiling now at every commonsense suggestion that once we see them from God's vantage point, we will know that the bad things that happen to us will turn out to be really good things in the long run. My heart—by which I mean my deepest moral feelings—will have none of my positive thoughts about unfair pain.

I must find another way to peace.

A few months ago I was waiting on the front porch of a tidy cabin on a rugged mountainside a few miles west of Buena Vista, Colorado, for my friend Els Ungvary to come to the door. I had come for one more visit with her husband, Sandor, before his ailing eighty-six-year-old body finally surrendered to its noble mortality. These two people could tell you about the horrible pain you can suffer when God lets you fall into the hands of evil men.

Els was Dutch. While working in the underground during World War II, she was once tied face down on a cement prison floor while Nazi storm troopers kicked and stomped on her back with their big, brown boots until they crushed her vertebrae. Sandor was Hungarian. While working in the underground, he was beaten and poisoned by the Nazis, and then, after the war, he was beaten again, imprisoned, and sentenced to be shot by the Communists. Talk about unfair pain! Yet in all the years I have known these people, I have never heard them wonder whether they could forgive God for letting such horrible things happen to them on his watch.

While I waited for Els to come to the door, I noticed a little brass cross nailed to the lintel, a dove engraved on the crosspiece. I thought it must tell me something about the way these two people lived their lives. It helpled explain why forgiving God had never entered their minds. They lived their lives pretty much the way Jesus lived his, doing what God called them to do, even though they had to pay a horrendous price to do it. But there is something else, I think, something deeper in their grasp of God.

When Jesus was crucified, the maker of the universe suffered everything that Jesus suffered. The same God who suffered with Jesus suffers with all of his children. He suffered with every child, every man and woman, in the death camps. He suffers when any of his children suffers at the hands of adults. Or when adults suffer at the hands of children. How can we forgive God for letting us suffer when he suffers more than we do?

I was taught early on in my life that God was above suffering. I now believe that suffering is his most typical way of being God.

At this point, common sense breaks in again, this time with doubts of its own. If God suffers when we suffer, he only compounds the suffering. To what end? Why would God choose to add his own pain to what is already a vast glut of pain? If he is suffering so much with us, he has all the more reason to make an end of it. This being the case, why does he not stop it for both our sakes? I have no answer to the question. I do not even want an answer.

I am done with common sense when it comes to finding

good reasons for not forgiving God. What I need more than a reasonable explanation of why we feel so much pain is simple courage to put out my hand and walk hand in hand through the suffering with my divine Fellow Sufferer. The question is: To what destination? The answer: To wherever he is leading us.

I have come to believe that the only workable response to unfair pain is hope. Hope for what? Hope for the time when pointless and unfair suffering no longer happens. In the crunch, when we see no clear evidence that this is where he is leading us, hope becomes a kind of courage. Courage to trust God with our hopes.

At this point, I must tell you about Etty Hillesum. She had the kind of courage I am talking about. Etty was a passionate, gutsy Jewish woman, only twenty-eight when she lived with a group of other young people in the Jewish section of Amsterdam in the bad days of 1942. Those were the days when the German army that was occupying the Netherlands began shipping Dutch Jews to the concentration camps. She and her friends had decided not to go into hiding, and the Germans kept tightening their grip on the city each day. All she could do was wait for the night when the Gestapo would pound on her door.

Etty kept a journal until the end, and just before she was jammed into a packed cattle car, Auschwitz bound, she tossed it to a friend. (Her journal was lost and forgotten until someone discovered it in 1986 and published it as a book called, in its English translation, *An Interrupted Life*.) At some point while waiting her turn to be taken away, Etty started reading the Bible, devoured it daily, discovered the Gospels, and developed a feisty faith in God. Her journal became a running conversation with him. And she put out her hand for God to take it and walk her through the troubles ahead.

I will quote a few sentences to give you a hint of her spiritual courage.

> From all sides our destruction creeps up on us and soon the ring will be closed, and no one will be able to come to our aid. . . .
> But I don't feel that I am in anybody's clutches: I feel safe in God's arms. . . . and whether I am sitting at my beloved old desk in the Jewish district or in a labor camp under SS guards . . . I shall feel safe in God's arms. . . .
> For once you have begun to walk with God, you need only keep on walking with him and all of life becomes one long stroll—such a marvelous feeling.

Was Etty Hillesum having religious delusions? I do not think so. I choose to believe that she had gotten hold of God in the one way that matters most when things go horribly bad for us.

And I feel no embarrassment to admit that after poking around in the world of faith all these years, I find myself longing for the faith and the courage of a twenty-eight-year-old woman who hardly had time to get the hang of true believing. It may be that God will give that faith to me, too, when the bad troubles come. And when he does, I shall simply take his hand and keep on walking at his side through the thick of those troubles. Perhaps, then, life, the good and the bad of it together, *will* become a stroll with God.

∾

Forgive God? If you feel you need to forgive him, it may do you some good to do it and get it over with. Just tell him you have to do it because you do not want to let your pain get between the two of you. I am sure he will accept your forgiveness in good grace and go on being your Fellow Sufferer. For myself, I do not have the heart for it. In spite of everything wrong he lets happen in our world, I cannot get myself to forgive the One who gives me every breath I breathe, forgives me every wrong I do, and suffers with every unfair pain I feel.

HOW WE FORGIVE

Fourteen
―――――――――

HOW GOD FORGIVES

G od invented forgiving as a remedy for a past that not
even he could change and not even he could forget.
His way of forgiving is the model for our forgiving. Forgive
each other the way God forgives us—this is what the Bible
says. How, then, does he forgive? And if we know, can we
do it the way he does? Considering the vast difference between us and the maker of the universe we may well wonder.
But we cannot be sure until we have a notion of how the
inventor of forgiving makes it work.

Jesus once told a beautiful story about how a Hebrew
father welcomed his son back home after the son had done
him wrong. It is such a favorite Bible story, I suppose, because it tells us that our heavenly Father takes us back after
we have done him wrong the way the father in the story took
his son back. The story has been retold thousands of times as
a story of forgiveness. Actually, it is about a family reunion.
And it tells us about forgiveness mostly by what it *does not* say
about it.

I suggest that we read the story again, the way we might
watch an old movie to see if there is something in it that we
had missed before.

THE ART OF FORGIVING

There was a man who had two sons. The younger one
said to his father, "Father, give me my share of the
estate." So he divided his property between them.

Not long after that, the younger son got together all
he had, set off for a distant country, and there
squandered his wealth in wild living. After he had spent
everything, there was a severe famine in that whole
country, and he began to be in need. So he went and
hired himself out to a citizen of that country, who sent
him to his fields to feed pigs. He longed to fill his
stomach with the pods that the pigs were eating, but no
one gave him anything.

When he came to his senses, he said, "How many of
my father's hired men have food to spare, and here I am
starving to death! I will set out and go back to my
father and say to him: Father, I have sinned against
heaven and against you. I am no longer worthy to be
called your son; make me like one of your hired men."
So he got up and went to his father.

But while he was still a long way off, his father saw
him and was filled with compassion for him; he ran to
his son, threw his arms around him and kissed him.

The son said to him, "Father, I have sinned against
heaven and against you. I am no longer worthy to be
called your son."

But the father said to his servants, "Quick! Bring the
best robe and put it on him. Put a ring on his finger
and sandals on his feet. Bring the fattened calf and kill
it. Let's have a feast and celebrate. For this son of mine
was dead and is alive again; he was lost and is found."
So they began to celebrate. (From Luke 15, author's
paraphrase)

There is more to the story. There is a sour brother who
grouses about the unfairness of it all, he with his nose to

duty's grindstone all the while, and never getting a thank you, let alone a dinner, while his no-good brother comes home to a banquet in his honor. I understand the complaining brother; he is the grump in me who is not impressed when celebrity prodigals get caught, exposed, converted, forgiven, and then quickly lionized as celebrity penitents. Oh, yes, I know the elder brother all right; he looks a lot like me.

But my issue is not with the faithful brother who needs no forgiveness. My focus is on the father who welcomed back the prodigal brother who did need to be forgiven. If we can get a notion of what was going on in the father's mind when he forgave his son, we will get a hint of what goes on when God forgives us. I will pry open the lid by asking five questions about the father's forgiving.

What did the father forgive his son for?

Forgiving, remember, is for people who have been both wounded and wronged by someone. If we are only wounded but not wronged, we may have no reason to forgive. If the prodigal son only hurt his father in some way, he needs to be explained, maybe excused, but not forgiven. So we need to understand how the father was wronged, if he was.

I have helped raise three rambunctious children, and I have felt some pain along the way that I never needed to forgive them for. And it seems to me that the prodigal caused his father some pain that needed no forgiving.

Take the matter of the money, for instance. From a legal viewpoint, the son asked only for what was his, no more. He did not steal it, and he didn't hire a lawyer to pry it out legally. The father put up no argument against his son getting it. He did not even moralize about how fools and their money are soon parted or sigh about the sharp teeth of a

119

son's ingratitude. He just forked it over: "It's your money, son. I'll have a cashier's check ready tomorrow."

Then, there's the taking off. Most fathers I know are embarrassed if their sons *don't* leave home. "Keep in touch, son, visit us now and then, but not to stay." Of course most fathers would think twice about turning over all that money in one lump sum to a son who had never earned a dollar of his own. Prudent fathers want to shield their children from the high price fools pay for freedom. This father, however, let the son take responsibility for himself, even though the odds on success were poor and the stakes in parental pain were high.

Out in the far country, as the older brother probably predicted, the young dolt plunged headfirst, eyes closed, into the demolishing of his own life. The script he played out was written for fools: bad crowd, no job, expensive partying, the whole bundle soon spent, and the "friends" gone when the cash went. Worse than being a sucker, the prodigal was a bore.

Things got even tougher. A drought, a depression, nothing for him but a rotten job feeding a goy's pigs. Still, feeding pigs is honest employment, if not all that gainful, so things could have been worse. At least a decent day's work seemed to clear his head enough for him to recognize the gap between the pleasant place he had left behind and the mess he had made of his life since he left it.

But being prodigal is not in the same basket with betrayal. It was something else that needed forgiving. And to get the feel of it, we need to look beyond our cultural beltline and put ourselves inside that ancient Hebrew family.

The prodigal did the worst thing a son could do to a Hebrew patriarch. In the Hebrew family every son was expected to serve the father until the time came for the son to be the caretaker of the father. So when his son grabbed whatever cash had been put away for him to inherit, thumbed his nose at the whole family, and headed off for God knew where without so much as a forwarding address, he was not just another grown-up son leaving home to carve out a life for himself. What he did was—for a Hebrew son—an offense in a class with killing his own father: "If a man has a stubborn and rebellious son . . . his father and mother shall . . . bring him to the elders at the gate of his town. . . . Then all the men of his town shall stone him to death" (Deut. 21:18–21). That was the law.

The family was the moral core of Hebrew life, and the father was the heart of the core. Stab the moral heart of the family, and you shed the lifeblood of the whole people. The prodigal did not merely disappoint his father as sons often do. He shamed him in the eyes of the neighbors and friends. But what was even worse was that he assaulted his father's God-ordained role. He was not just leaving the family; he was revolting against it. He was not only a prodigal; he was a rebel.

It wasn't the money. It wasn't the debauchery in the far country. It wasn't the disappointment of a son's failure to make a go of it. What this son did was the moral equivalent of patricide.

To separate the son's stupidity from his moral offense, I will offer another version of how the prodigal fared in the far country. In my version, he educated himself in finance and the cycles of nature, foresaw the coming drought, bought up storehouses full of grain, kept it undercover until disaster hit, got control of the international market, drove up prices, and made a fortune bigger than a small nation's yearly budget.

Getting rich on his own, he married a fabulously wealthy woman and more than doubled his estate. He took his wife home with him in a caravan attended by a hundred heathen slaves. The neighbors stood gawking in front of their farms. Once home, he invited his aging father to come live with him in the far country and have his own luxury apartment in the son's fifty-room palace, just the place to retire. What a son! What a pride!

My version of the story would have spoiled Rembrandt's magnificent portrayal of the prodigal's return. There would be no red-robed patriarch with moist eyes bending over and laying his long bejeweled hands on the threadbare back of the groveling deadbeat with sandals worn through to the bloody soles of his feet. The triumphant homecoming that I have suggested would have called for a Titian.

And would the son have needed to be forgiven if he came home in whooping triumph? Absolutely. Success abroad does not cancel out betrayal at home. Even if it involves a son who has become CEO of International Systems, Inc., betrayal could be honorably dealt with in one of two ways: Revenge it or forgive it. There were no other respectable options for a true Hebrew father.

When did the father forgive his son?

We cannot be sure, not exactly, but certainly it was while the son was not heard from out there in some far country. The father might have forgiven him long before the son thought up his penitent's speech. Certainly before he came shuffling home. Or the father may not have done it until a few minutes before he saw his son's haggard form stumbling down the path. Whenever it was done, inside the father's heart and mind, the son shuffled home forgiven in advance.

Forgiving done, all that was left was for the father to welcome his rebel home. Thus, when he saw the scruffy stalk stumbling down the dirt road a good ways down, the old man picked up the hem of his red robe in bent dignity, and loped to meet him, elbows flapping, galloping as no poised patriarch would ever be seen doing. And when he reached the son, the father threw his arms around his drooped shoulders, kissed his filthy cheek, and took him in.

The son wept at what a lout he had been and stuttered the speech he had prepared. "I have sinned, I deserve no more than a bunk in the barn." But the father paid no attention and gave no answer. It was not the time for confessions. Nor the time for blaming. Not even the time for forgiving. Time now for celebrating. Let's take off those rags, have a warm bath, put on a robe, declare a holiday, and pour the wine. The son is home.

When, then, did the father forgive his son? All we can say for sure is that there would have been no celebration if forgiving had not come some time before.

Now my third question:

Why did the father forgive his son?

If you had asked the father why he forgave his son, he might have shrugged off the question: "What else could I do? He's my son." He forgave his son because he loved him and wanted him back in the family, the only place for a Jewish son to be. He forgave his son for the son's sake and the family's sake. But for his own as well.

What if the prodigal had ended up on skid row in Sodom or homeless in Sidon and never came back? Just stayed away? Would the father have forgiven him had he never returned? We know that he forgave his son *before* the boy did in fact come back, so we may suppose he would have forgiven him had he never come back. This being so, we can also suppose that he must have forgiven the son for his own sake. Why else would he forgive a son who might never know he had been forgiven?

The father's life was less than half a life since the boy left home. His offended spirit had no peace. A whirlwind of pained resentment was blowing in his heart one day. Next day, the heart was a dark and dry, windless hole. He had to do something to save himself. So, alone, he cleared the decks of his spirit for the reunion he was not sure would ever happen. The father was no fool. Would he not have had the sense to heal his own spirit even if had no power to heal his son's?

How did the father forgive his son?

He did it the way anybody else, including God, does it. The first thing he did was to look beneath the offense into the reality of the offender. When the son closed the door and strutted off, all the father saw was an ungrateful son, a rebel, a fool, a traitor to the family. Then he moved his eyes off the wrong that the son did and began to look at the person his son was. He rediscovered the son inside the rebel, a foolish son, a guilty son, but his own loved son. With that look he rediscovered the humanity of his son and therewith took the first step of forgiving.

The second step was a decision not to demand the revenge that the law of Yahweh gave him a right to seek. Getting even with his own son was not for him. The instinct for judgment gave way to the impulse of love.

Now the third step. He longed for his son's good, at least for his safety and maybe his success in the far country, but most of all, for his coming home. But at home or away, let him be blessed. This was the finale, the sure sign that the work of forgiveness had been done. Now he could only yearn for the happy ending.

This story is mostly about the reunion. But there could have been no happy ending unless the father's forgiveness had done its healing work beforehand.

Now my final question:

Can we forgive each other the way the father forgave his son?

We forgive as we rediscover the person behind the offense, as we surrender our right to revenge, and as we wish good things for the person who did bad things to us, just as the father did. We can forgive before the person who does us wrong comes groveling back, as the father did. We can heal our own spirits, alone, and get the first benefits of forgiving, as he did. We can open ourselves to the possibilities of re-union, as he did.

But when it comes to the happy endings, we can never be sure.

Our prodigal does not always come home. He may hurt us and wrong us and never come back. We may need to forgive without ever hearing the crunching of stones beneath the sandals of a bone-weary wastral plodding to our door. For that matter, the last thing we may even want is for the person who wronged us to show up at our front door. If he pops in, we may tell him to move on. Maybe the family reunion would be a disaster for both of us, and we know it.

There is something unfinished about forgiving someone who does not come back to you, I give you that. The ending of the story Jesus told is the ideal way for things to go. But where we live, we cannot count on happy endings. We may have to heal our pain without healing the breach.

The Bible pictures God going through the same three basic stages when he forgives us that we ourselves go through when we forgive someone.

He rediscovers the humanity of the person who wronged him.

God covers up our sin the way a woman applies make-up over an ugly scar—so that she can look at her beauty without being put off by the blemish (Isa. 43:25 and Ps. 78:38). Or he bends over and picks the bad thing off our backs, carries it over to the ocean, and throws it away so he won't see us with sin on our backs (Mic. 7:19 and Ps. 103:1–3). Out of sight out of mind. Then again, he washes the dirt off our faces so that he can see us for what we *are* beneath the bad things we have *done* (Isa. 4:4 and Acts 22:16). In the gospel, God covers our sin with the blood that Jesus shed on the cross so he won't see our sin. Then again he washes us with the blood of the Lamb so that he can see the real us beneath our stains and can focus on the persons he made us and is remaking us to be. This is why "without the shedding of blood there is no forgiveness" (Heb. 9:22). In short, he covers up the wrong we *did* so that he can rediscover the persons we *are*.

He surrenders his right to get even.

Giving up vengeance is also a big part of divine forgiveness: "Yet he, being compassionate, forgave their iniquity, and did not destroy them" (Ps. 78:38 NRSV). The Bible tells us that vengeance belongs by right only to God. In forgiving he surrenders his right.

He wishes us well.

God invites all the thirsty, the hungry, and the prodigals whom he forgives back to their true home: "You shall go out in joy, and be led back in peace; the mountains and hills before you shall burst into song" (Isa. 55:12 NRSV). God sent his Son in the world so that through him "the world might be saved" (John 3:17 NRSV). The flagship word of the gospel is grace. No wonder, for grace is shorthand for God wishing us well. The will of the forgiving father is for all to be well with us and for all of us to be well.

Fifteen

OWNING OUR PAIN

Forgiving is a remedy for pain, but not for anybody else's pain, just our own. But no pain is really our pain until we own it. An odd notion, perhaps—how does one own pain?

Owning something is significantly different from possessing it. Possession is a legal arrangement. Ownership is a personal relationship. We possess something when we get hold of it in a way the law prescribes. We own something when we take personal responsibility for it. How do we do it? We take five basic steps.

First, we *appropriate* it. That is, we make something a property of ourselves, the way sweetness is a property of sugar or wetness of water.

We *acknowledge* it. We own up to ownership. We don't conceal it; we let people know that we are responsible for it. We are ready, if need be, to write our name on the front of it so that everybody who sees it will know who owns it.

We *name* it. Naming a thing gives it a special identity in the world. We name it so that anybody can know what it is and what it is for.

We *evaluate* it. We take stock of it, get a sense of its worth to us, decide how important it is to our lives, and what it would take for somebody to get us to part with it.

We take *responsibility* for it. We make ourselves accountable for what happens to it. We fix it if it is broken, buy insurance for it, pay taxes on it, and in general hold ourselves answerable for what happens to it while we own it.

Now we must move from owning *things* to owning *pain*. Here is an odd thing. Mostly we own things we deserve to have and want to keep. When it comes to unfair pain, we own what we did not deserve to get and do not want to have. So the question is: How do we own the pain we do not want?

Let's go back over the last five steps to ownership and point them in the direction of pain that we did not deserve to get, do not want, and need to be healed of.

We appropriate our pain.

We take our pain into our lives and let it settle into the persons we are. Once wounded, we become wounded people, and in some very deep ways we will forever be wounded people. The deeper our wounds, the deeper persons we can become—if we own the wounds.

I come from a line of Frisian Calvinists. Most Frisians, but especially my kind—farmers and blacksmiths—are intellectuals. This is why we prefer a tough intellectual religion like Calvinism. We put our brains in charge of our lives, and our brains do not even want to admit that we have feelings churning in the shadows beneath. We *have* the feelings, but we don't want to take them into our conscious selves. So being intellectual does not make us wise or smart.

About twenty years ago, a smart friend set me straight.

"Lew, you are the most feeling-driven person I have ever known."

"You are out of your mind," I said. "I am not driven by feelings. I am directed by reason."

"Hah."

So he showed me one thing after another about the way I react to the troubles of life and convinced me that I was indeed driven by feeling more than I was directed by reason. In fact, I learned that the more I disowned my feelings, the more they owned me in hidden and subtle ways I did not recognize.

He opened my eyes. I have stopped thinking of myself as a pure intellectual and have been happily or sadly, as the case recommends, learning to own my feelings and thus to own my pain.

We acknowledge our pain.

I watched my favorite uncle's face once while I stood by a tiny rectangular hole in the ground reading the burial service for his two-year-old grandson, a toddler whom he loved, I believe, with muted passion. Only family were there, all torn to pieces—except my uncle. Not a twitch in his face. No gulping. No squinting. No dropping of the head to hide tears. Nobody could have guessed that his heart was breaking.

At home, after the burial, I asked him how he stayed so dry, so controlled; I wanted to say so callous, so hard.

"These things happen," he said. "Nothing we can do. No point in falling apart."

Somewhere deep inside him, he was feeling a pain so terrible that his brain wanted to kill it before it killed him. I knew him well enough to know that. But he just would not acknowledge it. I think my uncle died with a compacted wad of disowned pain in his soul.

We name our pain.

Philosophers have said that the purpose of all education is to learn how to give things their right names. Naming something is a way of identifying it and distinguishing it from other things.

Feelings are sometimes hard things to name. Feelings flow in and out of each other like vapors, and they get mixed up and blended even as we feel them. They are "mushy, difficult, non-palpable, slippery things," Willard Gaylin wrote in his book *Feelings,* "difficult to distinguish within ourselves one from the other." Hard to brand, like a kicking steer.

But we need to name our pain when it comes to forgiving. We need to be able to identify our pain before we decide to forgive someone for it.

To show what naming pain is about, I will use the example of a gangly graduate student I shall call Jeff. He had recently secured one of his department's plumb assistantships, research assistant to Dr. Manifold Witness—a tenured and recognized scholar of American history and a man on the prowl for ever louder kudos from his guild. Jeff was finishing up his graduate research into Thomas Jefferson, whose line about all men being created equal is the creed of America's civil faith, but who owned slaves until he died.

Poking around forgotten papers tucked away in the archives, Jeff came on a small package of lost letters that Jefferson had written to Sally Hemmings, a beautiful young black woman, his slave, with whom, many thought, Jefferson had been having a love affair during his time in the White House.

Manifold Witness knew he was on to something big. He persuaded Jeff to postpone his graduation for a year and collaborate with him on the long-lost correspondence. Jeff would flush out the tension between Jefferson's secret passion for his slave and his public disapproval of slavery. Jeff would write a scholarly article about it and Witness would edit the final draft. They would be coauthors. Then Witness would see to it that it got published. Jeff's chances for a fine job at a good school had just taken a quantum leap forward.

At the next meeting of the American Historical Association, Manifold Witness read Jeff's paper. Manifold was introduced as the sole author. And his name was the only one under the title of the published copy. Jeff got a passing mention in a footnote.

Ask Jeff two questions. How does he size up what Manifold Witness has done to him? And what is it that he feels?

First, what Witness did:

"The crook *stole my work* from me."

Steal my work and you steal part of me.

Now let Jeff name his pain. He will stir his feelings around a bit, a slew of them swirling to the surface as he identifies the one he feels now:

I recognize annoyance, but, no, that's not what I *feel;* some disappointment, no, indignation, yes, but a lot more, too: grief, to be sure, but none of these is what I am feeling right now.

What I really feel is rage. My blood is boiling, and I hate that man. I wish he would get fired and die of frenzy on the spot.

I would say that the names he gave to his feelings pretty much match what Manifold did to him. They were understandable feelings for someone who has been cheated by a mentor he trusted. But the point here is that he was able to name them and by naming them, take a big step toward owning them.

THE ART OF FORGIVING

We evaluate our pain.

I recently heard a mother rage at the principal of a school in which her daughter, eleven, was about to enroll. She had just learned that her daughter would have to wear a uniform to school—the usual dark blue skirts and light blue blouses, with a red scarf loosely tied at the neck—no big expense either, not for this woman. Her beef was that her girl was required to wear the uniform at all instead of the pretty things her mother had bought for her. And the pain she felt was on the scale of the pain of someone whose mother had been mugged on Main Street.

Another mother felt outraged at the president of a small conservative college who had just expelled her son and sent him packing. What had her son done? He had confided to a friend that he had been smoking pot on weekends at his parents' cottage. He had trusted his friend to keep his confidence and asked for his support in his decision to quit. But his friend told the dean. The dean told the president. The president told the student to pack up and be off the campus that afternoon. His mother felt the pain of someone betrayed and flogged in the public square.

Most of us, I suppose, will agree that the woman whose daughter had to wear a uniform to school was feeling moral outrage when pique would have suited her. And most of us would also agree that the woman whose son was expelled from college was feeling an outrage suited to the case.

Some wrongs are worse than other wrongs. Some scratch the skin and others scour the soul. Some wrongs rate no more than pique and others rate outrage. To own our pain we need to give it the right value.

We take responsibility for our pain.

The pain that someone sticks us with asks us a simple question: What are you going to do with me? We did not want to get it, and we want to be rid of it. But we are stuck with it. We have to own it. And we begin to own our pain only when we respond to its question.

Before we answer, we can review our options. We can get even and make things worse by trying. We can try to forget it, stuff it into our subconscious where it will become a mole and do its mischief beneath the surface. Or we can forgive it and heal it. These are the options. Which one we choose is up to us. We cannot hand it over to a professional. We alone can answer the question our pains asks: Now that you are stuck with me, what are you going to do with me?

We begin to take responsibility for our pain when we listen to its question. We begin to heal our pain when we give the right answer.

∾

Let me sum up the simple point of this chapter. We will not take healing action against unfair pain until we own the pain we want to heal. It is not enough to feel pain. We need to appropriate the pain we feel: Be conscious of it, take it on, and take it in as our own. We need to acknowledge our pain, admit that we feel it, admit it to ourselves and to anyone else who wants to know. We need to name the pain we feel: Identify it for what it is and what it is not. We need to evaluate the pain we feel: Ask ourselves whether the pain we feel matches the kind of wrong we were done. And, finally, we need to take responsibility for the pain we feel: Decide what we are going to do with it—hold onto it, get even for it, or heal it.

When we have owned our pain, we are ready to do something else with it.

Sixteen

TAKING OUR TIME

I worry about fast forgivers. They tend to forgive quickly in order to avoid their pain. Or they forgive fast in order to get an advantage over the people they forgive. And their instant forgiving only makes things worse.

I am, of course, talking about forgiving serious wounds. If two people have a little late night spat and say some nasty things to each other, and one of them says she is sorry, let forgiving be done and to bed with them. We all suffer misdemeanors that hurt us some, but not gravely, and we do well to keep them in perspective, forgive them quickly, and carry on as before. But for serious wounds, we need to take our time.

When a normally sensitive person is betrayed by a person she trusted, she is diminished, treated like an object instead of a person. She may go into shock for a little while before she feels the wallop to her spirit, and shock may be a temporary pain-blocker. But if she forgives while she is still in shock, she is probably using forgiveness as a shield against the pain that is sure to come later.

Some people believe that anger is evil, and they forgive quickly to stifle their rage at the person who wronged them. A little pique or a mild indignation may be excusable, but a grand huff and puff is spiritually unseemly. Hurt badly enough to create a firestorm, they rush to forgive before they get burned by what they fear will become wicked rage.

Instant forgivers also say "I forgive you" as an escape from confrontation. Confrontation is so vulgar, so unpleasant, it's better to avoid it if at all possible. No ugly scene, please. Forgive him at once.

I worry most, however, about people who resort to fast forgiving as a trick to gain an advantage.

Quickly done, advantage gained, forgiving can be one of the smelliest of dirty tricks. In his play *A Doll's House,* Henrik Ibsen tells the story of a man whose wife got herself into a financial mess by overspending her allowance and piling up debts she could not pay to a banker who could have made things quite troublesome for him. But he forgave her—sweetly and swiftly forgave her—and by doing it, turned her into a plaster doll that he could display, coddle, use, and then put away again at his pleasure. By forgiving her, he possessed her. "It made her," explained Ibsen, "doubly his [possession]. . . . She has in a way become both wife and child to him."

People who have been wronged badly and wounded deeply should give themselves time and space before they forgive. My advice? Follow these five steps before you even begin to forgive.

Think: Come to as much clarity as you can on what actually happened. It takes time to get a focus on what actually happened.

Evaluate: Was it an accident? A misunderstanding? Or did he know what he was doing? Was it a lapse or has she made a career of lying to you? Did she merely annoy you, or did she truly wrong you?

Talk: Consult with a friend or counselor; get the help that the smartest of us need after we have been damaged.

Feel: Take time to be alone with yourself, without TV or tennis or chocolates or gabbing on the phone so that you can be in touch with what you feel. Besides, feelings are sloppy things, and it takes time to put a name on what it is we are feeling.

Pray: Forgiving is a tough act to perform when bad things are done to us. Here is a chance to be honest to God. Tell him how much it hurts, how full of hate you are. Admit you need help, ask for it, and use it when it comes.

There is one more reason for waiting before we forgive. The situation may not be ripe for it. We are hard put to forgive someone who is still battering us. When Dietrich Bonhoeffer, pastor and martyr in Hitler's Germany, was sitting in prison, he wondered some about forgiving. He concluded that forgiveness would have to come, "or we shall all be destroyed," but not yet, not until "violence has become justice, lawlessness become order, and war has become peace" (in *Letters and Papers from Prison*).

A dozen years ago, when Nelson Mandela, the first president of the Republic of South Africa, was still in prison, and people could only hope against hope for change, I mentioned to a black leader of that land that I was writing a book about forgiving.

"Ah, yes, forgiving," he said, "it will have to come to that sometime, but not yet, not while the boot is still on our neck."

But don't wait too long.

If it is risky to forgive too quickly, it is even more hazardous to wait too long.

If we wait too long to forgive, our rage settles in and claims squatter's rights to our souls. Our resentment gets into our bloodstream and is as hard to get out as a spoonful of ink from a glass of water. Our rage weaves itself into the texture of our spirits. We become the pain we feel. We cannot cleanse ourselves of it without loss to our own identity.

I know a man of seventy who says he was cheated out of a promised retirement bonus fifteen years ago. He knows for sure who did it. It was the new vice president in charge of personnel. Everyone who has spent more than fifteen minutes with him has heard the story. Every taxi driver who has driven him more than two miles knows it; the postman knows; the woman at the checkout counter knows. His rage has become his very being.

He *is* his bitterness. He breathes it, sleeps with it, and will probably die with it. In fact, he may die *of* it; the poison has splattered his organs, and an ulcer now bleeds on the lining of his once healthy stomach. He has waited too long. If he forgave he would not know who he was. He could still do it, and maybe he will, but his postponements have made it dreadfully hard.

☙

There is a right moment to forgive. We cannot predict it in advance; we can only get ourselves ready for it when it arrives. I have no more precise directions for picking the right time than this unscientific advice: Don't do it too quickly, but don't wait too long. How fast is too fast? How slow is too slow? Nobody can tell us ahead of time. Only the hurting person can know for sure when the time has come. The wise will act when it has.

Seventeen

WE DON'T HAVE TO
SAY SO

When we believe we've finally done it, we may have
an itch to tell the person who wounded us that she
is forgiven. We may feel that we are cheating on the process if
we don't. Or we may tell her and then wonder why she does
not dance a jig to celebrate our tender mercies.

Our ideal forgiving script might look something like this.
Jack has been in a stew about the rotten thing Jill did to him.
He is the most miserable of fellows until he decides to forgive
her. He thinks he has almost done it and runs to tell her:
"I've forgiven you, darling. It's all forgiven and forgotten."
Jill erupts with hilarious joy, throws herself on Jack, and
kisses him, and they are living happily ever after—for the
time being.

A happy ending for sure. But we should not suppose that
we must tell. Silent forgiving can be just as real and just as
effective as spoken forgiving.

Many years ago, I hurt two people whom I admired as
much as I admired anyone in the world. It was something I
said about them. They were the last two people in the world
whom I would have wanted to wound. But what I said badly
and needlessly wounded them. They asked me to meet them

for lunch. I went. They looked me in the eye and said: "We shall never forgive you. Never."

For almost fifteen years, I lived with the shame and sorrow of having hurt someone I loved and admired. Then one day I became very ill, and they seized the chance to contact me, wish me recovery, and express their concern. One thing led to another, letters back and forth, a visit, long talks on the phone, a still longer visit, and our friendship came alive again. I cannot think of many things in my life that I am more grateful for.

They have never said, "We forgive you." But I know they have. We do not need words.

There are two good reasons why silent forgiving is sometimes better than spoken forgiving. One of them is that not all of us have a talent for telling people that we forgive them. The other reason is that the people we forgive are not always ready to hear us. What they hear may cross paths with what we say, collide, and end up trashing our good intentions. As, for instance, when these two alienated brothers got together.

"I forgive you."

"What was that you said?"

"I said that I forgive you."

"You forgive me? What for? What did I ever do to you?"

"You cheated me, that's what you did. You grabbed a chunk of Mother's inheritance that she meant for me. You know you did."

"I cheated you? Let me tell you about cheated. I got cheated. That's who got cheated. Who took care of Mother when she needed it? Who did her bookkeeping for her? Who got her into a good nursing home? Who visited her every Saturday afternoon for five years? Talk about forgiving me? You are the one who needs to be forgiven."

"She meant to leave me half of the estate. You and your lawyer got her to change her will when she wasn't all there in her head and you ended up with getting two-thirds of all she had."

"So that's why you haven't said a word to me. You've been brewing a vat of resentment against me and never so much as said a word."

"I didn't resent you; I was just hurt."

"You were not hurt; you were just spiteful. That's all it was—pure spite."

"Well, just remember that it was I who did the forgiving."

"Yes, and I will never forgive you for forgiving me."

Good intentions badly botched. Some of us have no talent for talking; better if we keep quiet.

Let me offer ten tips that I have given people bent on telling other people that they are forgiven. If these tips look helpful, keep them for later reference. If not, read them and forget them.

1. *Take your time.* When you think you are ready to talk about it, postpone it for at least a week, or better two or three, while you go over all the possibilities a few more times.

2. *Size up the risk.* Forgiving is a sure thing. Talking about it is a gamble. You are as capable as the next person of messing it up. So assess your tolerance for risk before sharing your good news.

3. *Wait for a signal.* What sort of signal? People have many ways of signaling to us that they are ready to hear words of forgiveness. If you are blessed, he will tell you right out that he is sorry for what he did. Then again, he may just send you a Christmas card. Any signal will do.

4. *Do it sideways.* Be oblique. Talk about other things first. What things? Things that concern him. Maybe he's worried about something—his children, the stock market, his blood pressure. Or maybe he needs congratulations for doing something fine you've heard about. Listen for a while. Get to forgiving later, as if it were an afterthought.

5. Begin at the end. All forgiving hits its stride when a wounded person wishes good things for the person who did bad things to her. I suggest that we begin the conversation there. When you start by wishing him well, and do it with conviction, you are actually telling him you forgive him even though you haven't yet said the magic word.

6. Don't claim holy motives. Nobody wants to be forgiven just so that you can claim credit with God. If you give the impression that you are forgiving because you are trying to be a good person, you make it harder for someone to take your forgiving as a gift.

7. Improvise. Nobody responds exactly the way we think he or she should. So do it the way good jazz players do. Improvise; wait for the other person to respond in his own words, and then respond to his response.

8. Make it short. Say "I forgive you" once and let it go at that. If you repeat it, you make it sound as if you don't believe the other person heard it. And you may force him to reply before he is ready.

9. Keep it light. Angels fly because they take themselves lightly, said G. K. Chesterton. So do conversations about forgiving. Don't be weighty. And for goodness sake don't get blubbery.

10. Give the other person time. He has his own clock. Change the subject quickly if you sense he isn't ready to talk. Let him think about it. It isn't easy for him either. Maybe he won't mention it again, leave you wondering for a while. Once you say it, let him walk at his own pace.

My strategies are meant for people who forgive and want to initiate the conversation on their own. If the other person comes to you, however, and begs for your forgiveness, you don't need any strategy. You follow your heart. Say what you feel. You can hardly go wrong as long as you are honest. Maybe you'll say you need some time. Maybe you'll say, "Of course, I forgave you long ago." Maybe you will forgive on the spot. The point is simply that if the other person does come with sorrow in his heart and regrets on his lips, it is always good to forgive and never bad to say so.

My ten tips need a final point. Spoken forgiving, no matter how heartfelt, works best when we do not demand the response we want. I mean that when we tell people we forgive them, we must leave them free to respond to our good news however they are inclined. If the response is not what we hoped for, we can go home and enjoy our own healing in private.

Eighteen

WE DON'T HAVE TO
PUT UP WITH IT

Her rage pinched her voice into a hiss as she defied me to tell her how she could forgive a creature who had done the worst thing to her that anybody could ever do to a mother. A man who had just moved into a house down the street from hers got drunk one night four months ago, fought with his wife, got into his Lexus, gunned it past her house, struck down her four-year-old boy, left him dead on the curb at the edge of her front lawn, and drove away.

"Forgive him?" she wheezed. "Better he burn in hell."

I had never felt more respectful awe at a woman's fury. It happened on a radio talk show. Ten minutes later, another woman called.

"I heard the woman whose boy had been murdered," she explained, "and I knew I had to call and tell you my story because the same thing happened to me four years ago."

It turned out that her boy, too, was just four years old, that he had been struck by a drunk truckdriver, dragged fifty yards, and killed. She had never really known before how powerful hate could make a person feel. Hate became her inner heat, its flame refueled each time a lumbering truck rumbled past her house. Every day that dawned, she ordered the Great Avenger to stomp his heel on this worm. Hate was her only strength. For a while.

Then it turned against her and began to choke her by degrees. After two years of captivity to her hate, she woke up to the fact that the man who killed her son was killing her. And she was giving him permission.

What could she do to reclaim her life? See a therapist? Maybe. But why not try her priest first? The good father's first impulse was to push her straight into the religious solution, that her salvation lay in forgiving the man. But then good sense got to him.

He said: "Before we do anything at all, you and I have to start a chapter of Mothers Against Drunk Driving in our town. You have to let this town—and yourself in the bargain—know that you are mad as a hornet and are not going to tolerate drunk driving. After that we can talk about forgiving."

They did it. She gradually backed into forgiving in the strength of intolerance and came back to life. This was her story. I do not know whether the first woman heard it or what she thought of it if she did. But it makes my point: Forgiving intolerable things does not make them tolerable.

Forgiving starts out on the premise that some things are intolerable and that nobody should tolerate them. They are intolerable, not because we have no stomach for them, but because they violate the law of life. It is precisely because they are intolerable that such a radical remedy as forgiving had to be found for them.

Any community of people with diverse beliefs about what is tolerable has to negotiate what it can put up with. We all have to put up with some things that we believe the community ought not tolerate. But our putting up with them does not mean that we think they are tolerable.

It is a sticky thing, this business of putting up with what we believe is intolerable. It gets stickier still when it comes to forgiving the intolerable things people do to us. So before we go on, I want to stake out a few nonnegotiable assumptions about forgiving and tolerance.

Some things are intolerable in and of themselves no matter how many people put up with them.

Intolerable things are forgivable.

Forgiving an intolerable wrong does not make it tolerable.

Forgiving an intolerable thing does not mean we intend to put up with it.

With these nonnegotiable premises in hand, we can poke around a bit more in the art of forgiving intolerantly.

What sorts of things should we not tolerate? Any morally healthy person knows them when she experiences them, but it can't hurt to mention a few. Cheating on a partner is intolerable. So is abusing a child. Or lying to a friend. Forcing sex on a person who does not want it is intolerable. So is racism. Such things are intolerable under all conditions, in all cultures, all times. They do not become tolerable whenever a certain number of muddleheaded people decide to tolerate them. They would be intolerable if everybody on earth tolerated them.

Remember that forgiving was invented precisely as a remedy for the wounds that intolerable wrongs leave us with. When somebody does something really horrid to us, we may explode: "That is unforgivable." But we don't mean it. What we may mean is: "What you did to me is so intolerable that I will never be able to forgive you for it." But the fact that you or I do not have the grace or the wisdom to forgive something does not make it unforgivable any more than my inability to speak Nepalese makes Nepalese unspeakable.

Let me tell you a simple story that I think illustrates the differences between forgiving and tolerating something.

Daphne is a long-suffering woman who put up too long with a freeloading boyfriend named Matt. Not only would he have nothing to do with marriage, Matt did not have a job and did not work hard at finding one. She had hoped that he would soon be earning some money and showing some promise for the future, but nothing ever turned up that matched his skills or met his terms. Finally Daphne began to wonder whether he really wanted a job, and a notion, quickly chucked, did cross her mind that maybe he was using her.

The fact was that she used him; he gave her a companionship that made up, most of the time, for his lack of promise. So Daphne stayed in the relationship. He was harmless, and she could at least trust him, which was more than she could say for some other males in her past. So, given the trade-off, she figured she could put up with his preference for hanging around over gainful employment.

Then the plot took on a darker color.

The manager of her apartment stopped her outside the parking lot one night, took her aside, and told her that a couple of police officers had been asking questions about the lady who visits with Matt a couple afternoons a week. A few days later, Daphne discovered that Matt had been using her ATM card to get cash. Now what she had been putting up with suddenly became intolerable.

Daphne threw Matt out—the reflex action of someone who knew the difference between putting up with an unemployed lout and tolerating a cheating louse. Cutting him off did not satisfy her; she wanted to get even, and as most revenge seekers do, she settled for lonely fantasies like slicing off his ears while his drug-dealing girlfriend watched. But even while she was getting even with Matt in her fantasies, she knew she was really raging against herself.

Daphne resorted to a spiritual counselor who was smart enough not to push her into quick forgiving. She persuaded Daphne to congratulate herself for the strength she had to kick Matt out of her life. And persuaded her that she was her own basic problem and that she needed first of all to discover that she was a good enough person for far better men than Matt. And finally, in a cagey, unspiritual style, the counselor suggested that forgiving Matt for the intolerable things he did to her might clear the deck for dealing with the wounds she had inflicted on herself.

Not everyone clobbered by intolerable wrongs can rid herself of the Matts in her life. People are sometimes captives in tragic situations; they have no choice but to put up with wrongs that are intolerable. They face the ultimate question of a long-suffering spirit: *Can we put up with intolerable wrongs done to us and save our own souls in the very act of putting up with them?*

Many of us have been awed by stories of how ordinary human beings became almost divine in their power to transcend the intolerable barbarity of concentration camps. One story that staggers me is about Agnes, a tall, thin, erect woman who found herself mired in the Austrian camp at Malthausen, a labor camp, not a camp equipped for slaughter but one where prisoners were sometimes worked to death and treated like animals in the process.

Agnes was fated to come under the power of a squat, pimpled sergeant named Bernard who elected her to be his private victim. He leered while he watched her take showers, prodded her with his rifle barrel at every roll call, poked obscene finger gestures in her face, and whispered that he was going to rape her one night. She would have put a knife in his back if she had had one. But she determined not to let this evil man destroy her spirit.

So she made an outlandish decision: She would try to save herself by trying to forgive him. She began by looking for signals that there really was a human being—albeit a pitiful, weak, vulgar, shamed human being—beneath the skin of the snake. She found signals. She caught a glimpse of him once hanging his head down and putting his arm over his eyes while his fellow guards taunted him for being a slob. Once she caught a glimpse of him smiling at a little child and slyly giving her a piece of bread. Paltry proof of humanity, but she grabbed it.

She disciplined her imagination and surrendered her dreams of revenge. And finally she actually made prayers on his behalf. She prayed that the maker of the universe might redeem his soul. She was never sure she wanted what she was praying for, but she prayed nonetheless, and gradually, to her own silent amazement, discovered that she was meaning what she prayed.

Forced to endure the worst of all that is intolerable, she actually began to forgive the beast. She did what few forgivers can do: She began to forgive him while suffering the very thing she needed to forgive. Perhaps she had to; it was then or never. She might well be dead before the week was out. So she took control of her own soul by forgiving a monster hellbent on destroying it. But never for a moment, in her own mind, did Agnes suppose that forgiving her private Nazi terrorist somehow changed his intolerable bestiality into something humanly tolerable.

When I try to put myself in Agnes's place, I would not bet a nickel on my courage or grace to do what she did. I cannot even understand how she did it. But what she did teaches one all-important truth about forgiving: Forgiving and tolerating have nothing in common. They live in different worlds.

Forgiving may enable us to bear up under and even to surmount intolerable abuse that people do to us when we cannot escape it. But it can never, should never, shall never, transform intolerable wrong into tolerable pain.

Nineteen

HOW OFTEN? AS OFTEN AS WE NEED TO

Peter—Christ's pushy apostle—wondered how long the unbridled forgiving that Jesus seemed to be recommending was supposed to go on. Suppose a recidivist liar cheats me once or twice and then says he's awfully sorry. I forgive him, and then he reverts and cheats me again. And again.

"How many times am I supposed to forgive him, Jesus? Pick a number, seven for example. Should I forgive him seven times?"

Peter was asking a hypothetical question. So Jesus gave him a hypothetical answer. "Not only seven times but seventy times seven."

But Claudia was not being hypothetical when she asked the same question recently. Her husband, a clown named Clarence, had been beating on her for some time. Her minister has told her that Jesus tells us to forgive seventy-times-seven times. Clarence sees to it that she has plenty of chances. After he has pummeled her some, he puts on his sackcloth, solemnly promises that he will never touch her again, and begs her to forgive him. She does. But the very next time he has had a few drinks he wallops her again. And begs her to forgive him again. Which she does. Until now. Now she wonders how many times she is supposed to do it.

Claudia believes that as an obedient wife she owes it to Clarence to keep on doing what Clarence wants her to do. Clarence wants her to forgive him. If she stops forgiving Clarence, she fears God will stop forgiving her. Better to be damaged by Clarence than damned by God. So with God in his corner Clarence has the advantage. But is there a limit? Claudia wants to know.

Before getting more involved with Claudia's troubles, let's slip back to Peter's conversation with Jesus. Peter wanted to know how often a person was supposed to forgive a repeat offender. Jesus refused to take Peter's question seriously; he put Peter on a bit, saying, in effect, "If you want me to reduce forgiving to a numbers game, try these numbers for size: Forgive, not seven times or seven times seven times, but seventy times seven."

Ask a silly question, get a silly answer. The point is, don't be a scorekeeper. You miss the whole point if you do. The wild number Jesus threw out was his way of saying that we frustrate the entire healing process if we calculate the number of times we are duty bound to do it.

Forgiving is not like pulling up our bait after we have caught our limit of fish. Nor is it like a judge who lets thugs off the first two times, but on a third offense, locks them up for keeps. Numbers are not in the forgiving calculus.

Now back to Claudia. The very fact that she wants to know how many times she must forgive Clarence is a hint that she has misunderstood what forgiving is all about. To get rid of the "how often" bogey, she would do well to take stock once more of three fundamental facts of forgiving:

Forgiving is not an obligation.

"How many times?" is what legalists want to know. But forgiving is an opportunity to do something good for ourselves after somebody has done something bad to us. Why fret about how often duty requires us to do ourselves some good?

Forgiving is not about letting people get away with something.

Let it be shouted once more, from the roof this time: Forgiving a person does not mean that we tolerate what that person is doing to hurt us. Forgiving does not turn us into mush.

Forgiving is not about staying with people who are hurting us.

Forgive a wife-slammer if you can. But you don't have to live with him. Forgive a husband who is abusing your children if you can. But only after you kick him out of the house. And if you can't get him out, get help. It's available. In the meantime, don't let him near the kids, and don't let anyone tell you that if you forgive him it means you have to stay with him.

I repeat these three fundamental points because when people ask how often they should forgive, what they usually want to know is how much abuse they need to put up with. They are not really asking about forgiving. They are asking about tolerating. And they need to understand that forgiving and tolerating are different species, as different as cantaloupes and basketballs.

We certainly need to set limits. But not on forgiving. It is abuse we need to set limits on. How much of this should we take? No more, certainly, than we have already taken. But to be decisive about this in real situations, we also need to be realistic about what is actually going on.

What is really going on may be insufferable abuse. It may also be sufferable annoyance. Or it may be annoyance with intent to abuse. In real life only the victim knows, and she cannot always tell for sure. This is why we need a nose for the difference. And if we lack it, we need the help of people with clearer vision than ours.

Let's take another look at an abuse situation.

Say you have innocently—probably foolishly—let a thug into your life disguised as a needy lover. He has the body of a brute. You are a wisp of a thing. So you cannot prevent him from abusing you.

How many times should you forgive your household bruiser? You should not even think about forgiving him. Not yet. Not as long as he has his foot on your neck. Your problem at this point is not forgiving. Your problem is how to get out of his reach. Once you get away from him, you can think about forgiving him. And then the question of how *often* to forgive him will be obsolete. You will have enough on your hands to do it just once.

But revise my household tragedy and make it a tragicomedy. Say that your husband has been needling you with irritating routines that, by themselves, you can put up with—up to a point. He ignores you at parties while he talks office politics with a statuesque beauty from the secretarial pool. He makes snide jokes about your minister in front of your friends from church. He picks his nose with one hand and clutches a beer can with the other while he watches football and then falls asleep on the sofa as soon as the game is over. Things like that.

No single one of his offenses matches any of the bruises an abused wife suffers. But let them accumulate, and they add up to more than mere buffoonery. What he does to you ties your upper intestine into a Dutchman's knot because you have a hunch that what is going on here is not just personal failings but calculated contempt. His needling is a prickly code for his—his what? His scorn, his contempt, yes, and his sickly need to cut you down a notch or two.

The real question is not how many times to forgive, but what is really going on here, and how much can you put up with? If his petty annoyances are camouflaged abuse, your problem is how to get him to face up to what he is doing, why he is doing it, and when he is going to quit. Once he comes to his senses, you can think about forgiving. But when you do, don't let him think for a split second that forgiving him is a signal that you are ready to put up with his piggish ways.

You may have more than ample capacity to accommodate the daffiness of people you have to live with. But you also know that there is a limit. At some point, good humor ends and putting down of feet begins. So you tell him that his piddling irritations give you serious pain and that you want him to stop it.

What Jesus said about forgiving seventy times seven had nothing to do with putting up with things until the seventy times eighth offense. He was telling us not to make forgiving a matter of numbers. He was talking about healing our memories of a wound that someone's wrong etched in our cemented past. Once we have stopped the abuse, we can forgive however many times that it may take us to finish our healing.

Back to Peter's question. It was simply the wrong question, and to give a straight answer to it would have been to give it a standing it did not deserve. The question is never how many times we are *supposed* to forgive, but how many times we *need* to forgive. Forgiving is a gift, not a duty. It is meant to heal, not to obligate. So the only good answer to Peter's question is: Use the gift as often as it takes to set you free from a miserable past you cannot shake.

Twenty

WHEN WE ARE
NOT SURE WE HAVE
DONE IT

When my wife, Doris, and I crossed beyond middle age, we counted our money and decided that we should salt some of it away in an IRA for the day of our retirement. We talked about it to an honest broker who told us: "Conservative mutual funds are the thing for folks like you. I have my own mother in one of them. Let the professionals do the work for you." We did it and rested smug until, a few years down the road, the devil pushed the stock market down a black hole, and being new to the quirks of equities, we wondered whether our retirement was in freefall to destitution.

"Hang steady," our broker advised us. "What goes down eventually comes up. Look at the record. Take the long view. Stay the course."

People who have been hurt and have forgiven the person who wounded them are a little like long-term investors. Their investment in healing usually grows, even with all dividends reinvested, in modest increments. There is turbulence along the route, too, and forgivers can get to feeling that their investment in forgiving was a sucker's choice. Sometimes they wonder whether they really have forgiven at all.

People have said things like these to me:

"I discover that I don't like the person I thought I had

163

forgiven anymore than I did back when he cheated me. In fact I really dislike him a lot."

"I still get steaming angry when I think of what he did to me."

"I don't feel comfortable when he comes around; he showed up the other day and wanted to take me to lunch, and I realized I didn't want him to get near me."

"I still feel pain when I remember what happened. Shouldn't the hurt have gone away by now?"

"I heard that his new wife left him, and I couldn't get myself to feel bad."

They report experiences like these because they wonder whether they have failed at forgiving. I give them some advice that I will pass along here. If what I say to them is helpful to you, so much to the good. If you don't need it, even better. But here it is.

Be patient.

Recall that forgiving does not usually happen at once. It is a process, sometimes a long one, especially when it comes to wounds gouged deep. And we must expect some lapses, the way long-term investors expect some downs in the market. When it happens, stay the course. And look on the downside as an opportunity to reinvest, do it again, get back in practice.

There is a line in a hymn they used to sing in the hill country that celebrates the way divine forgiving closes the books on all charges against us.

> *The old account was settled long ago, long ago,*
> *Long ago, Long ago,*
> *Praise God, the old account was settled long ago.*

Good for God. He can forgive and be done with it. That is reassuring to know. But ordinary people are not always able to settle accounts once for all the way he does. True enough, some people seem to manage to finish off forgiving in one swoop of the heart. But when they do, you can bet they are forgiving flesh wounds. Deeper cuts take more time and can use a second coat.

Religious people, more than others maybe, expect to complete the project quickly, particularly after they have asked God to help them. With his help, they think, they should get it done on the spot and perfectly at that. What they forget is that God himself tends to baffle us with his patience about things we want done now. He is, for instance, taking his own sweet time getting the world to work right. Why should we be surprised, then, that creatures of time like us should need some time to do the difficult job of healing our wounded memories?

Sometimes it is the fault of the person we have forgiven. He shows up out of nowhere, and the sight of him scratches the scar open, and the old account seems quite unsettled again. Sometimes it is our own doing. We turn on the old tape while we lie awake at night and listen to it over and over again, like rubbing our tongues on a canker sore while we complain about how much it hurts.

Even in the best of circumstances, however, forgiving serious injuries needs patience. Where I live there is a section of Interstate Highway 5 that Californians call the Grapevine, a slow grade to about five thousand feet. It's not all that high, but it is a wearisome climb that exasperates me considerably. The road levels off deceptively at several points and tricks me into thinking I have gotten over the crest. Then I feel gypped when I discover I have more to go. I am never sure when I really have gotten to the top until after I have gotten over it a bit and the Toyota surges to the touch of my foot. Forgiving is often like this—a slow haul up a long incline. And we are often not sure we are over the hump until one day we feel a lightness in our spirits that was too long in coming.

165

My broker had it right. We are invested for long-term growth. When the turbulence from past pain comes back, the only thing for it is to stay on course. Hang patient. Forgiving, like all creative spiritual ventures, takes time.

Expect some relapses.

Early on in her marriage, a lovely woman I know let the man she unwisely married persuade her that she was ugly and useless and that she deserved every demeaning insult he slung at her. He pounded her ego down a notch every morning on rising and another notch on going to bed. Then she was given eyes to see her own worth, her own dignity, and her own beauty, which is another story, but it led her to stop putting up with his abuse. And when he would not quit, she left him. Later on she forgave him, set herself free from the hateful misery he left her with, and went on to become a successful and reasonably happy person.

Two decades after she left him, she heard that her former husband had had a heart attack. A cool wave of suspicious satisfaction washed up on her spirit: *Serves him right,* she thought. *Maybe God is finally getting him for what he did to me.* Caught off guard by the revival of her spite, she had a talk with me.

"What is the matter with me? I thought I forgave him. Years ago. But how could I have such feelings if I actually forgave him?"

"Nothing is the matter with you. You are having a little relapse. Happens to most of us."

"So what do I do now?"

"Do what you did the first time. Say it. Say it to yourself. Say it out loud. You're better at it now than you were then; it should be easier this time."

She did and it was. Words are not where forgiving happens. But words are catalysts. They warm us up for the doing of what we say. Then they reinforce our intention to keep doing it. Saying "I promise" helps us keep the promises we make. And saying "I forgive" again energizes us to do it again. In short, a relapse is not failure; it is a new opportunity.

Stay angry.

Sometimes people wonder how they could have forgiven someone when they are still angry at what she did. My response is: If you feel angry about what happened to you, congratulate yourself. Your anger is a clear sign that you are in touch with reality. If you weren't angry you would have lost one of the best parts of being human.

If you still get angry after you forgive, let your anger protect you from being a sucker for similar wounds in the future.

Forgiving is not anti-anger, anymore than love is anti-anger. Recall, if you are a parent, how steamed you can get at your toddler for getting into the same mischief for the eleventh time. Recall how, even while you sputter, you want all the blessings stored in heaven to fall on his lovely head. And if his mischief landed him in danger, you would walk through fire to pull him out. In the same way, you can be angry at what the person you forgive did to you and still wish him well. Not in the same breath, maybe, but on the second or third.

The enemy of forgiving is hate, not anger. Anger is aimed at what persons do. Hate is aimed at persons. Anger keeps bad things from happening again to you. Hate wants bad things to happen to him. Anger is the positive power that pushes us toward justice. Hate, by that token, is the negative force that pushes us toward vengeance. Anger is one of love's good servants. Hate serves nobody well. So if you get angry when you remember what he or she did to you, it does not mean that you have not forgiven him. It only means that you get mad when people do bad things to you.

We don't have to like him.

One woman said that her ex-husband had been sending her signals that he would like to get back together with her. In her fogged-in past he had left her a note on the refrigerator door one day and slipped off to Las Vegas with his "one true" love. The new marriage did not last, so he tried another, and now, after three divorces, he was alone again, chastened, and at her door and asking to be taken in again.

"When he came to see me," she said, "I woke up to the fact that I don't even like him, maybe I never did. I don't wish him any harm. I had really hoped his last marriage would last. But when he is around me, I just wish he would go away."

She disliked him thoroughly, did not want to spend the time of any day with him, did not want to talk with him, work with him, or play with him, and she told him to go away. What is more she liked disliking him. But she wondered whether not liking him meant that she had not forgiven him.

I did not understand why she imagined that a woman of her good taste should expect herself to like someone who leans so inerrantly toward crudity and wrongdoing. Forgive him? Yes. Like him? Why would she? He is not a likable creature.

The likable people are the tricky ones. They tempt us to confuse liking with trusting. They come back after we have forgiven them in their devilish likableness, slither their way into our backyards, and then cheat us, betray us, even brutalize us again before we know what they are up to. Cheaters are likely to be likable; being liked is their entree into their victim's trust. But forgiving them does not mean we have to be dumb enough to trust them the second time around.

We all need a little help.

Friends can help us most if they are honest friends and have a little insight. If you don't have such a friend, you can look for the right kind of minister or priest or rabbi. Many of them are smarter about forgiving than therapists are. But avoid any minister who tries to get you to forgive on grounds that it is your duty and then tells you that if you do forgive you are expected to go back into the relationship that was abusive to you before.

The best source of help can be found in a group of fellow strugglers. There are plenty of them about because not many people get far in life without having been wounded unfairly. Just being with people who are fighting the good fight against painful memories assures us that we are not alone. And getting to know people who are succeeding—albeit in fits and starts—at their own healing always revives our courage to hang in with the forgiving we started.

We are all confused after we get hurt. Getting wounded and being wronged always skew our vision of what happened and how we let it happen to us. Forgiving does not clear everything up. We need sometimes to wash the mirror of our memories, and we may need someone to lend us a sponge.

∾

Forgiving is the hardest chord to play in the human concerto. Few of us are naturals. Most of us are pluggers. And after we have done it a few times, we can lose our touch again and backslide now and then. But a backslide is not a failure. It's only a slip on the way to success.

Twenty-one

FORGIVE AND REMEMBER

Forgiving is a way of solving the first of two persistent problems that have forever bedeviled the human spirit: We were given the remarkable power to remember and were given no power to change what we remember. We could live happily with this condition if our pasts were all happy. But it becomes a severe problem to us when the past we cannot change and must remember is a painful past when we were wounded and wronged by someone we trusted.

Forgiving does not erase the bitter past. A healed memory is not a deleted memory. Instead, forgiving what we cannot forget creates a new way to remember. We change the memory of our past into a hope for our future.

In this way, we also solve the second persistent problem of the human spirit. The second problem, like the first, is created by a combination of a power and weakness, both of them native to our spirits. The power is our ability to imagine the future. The weakness is our inability to control the future. The answer to the problem of imagining a future we cannot control is hope. And the way to hope for a better future after a bad past is the way of forgiving.

How does it work? Let me suggest a few ways.

We remember the good parts of the bad past.

We see the bad things that happened in the past through the lenses of whatever good has come to us afterward.

Why do we build memorials to bad times, and why do we travel across the country to see them? Do we visit the Holocaust Museum or the Vietnam Memorial to wallow in the horror of those tragic events? I don't think so. I think we build monuments to bad things for three reasons: to keep alive our memories of the good people who suffered them, to revive our gratitude that we were delivered from them, and to renew our resolve that we shall not let such horrors afflict the human family again.

The biblical story of Joseph is a touching example of how a memory of a bad thing is turned into the beginning of a good thing. Joseph's older brothers were jealous of him because he was their father's favorite. The last straw came when he told them a dream he had in which he had become their master and they had become his servants. So they conspired to sell him off, a mere boy, as a slave to wandering nomads. The nomads then sold him to a man of influence in the Pharaoh's court who introduced him to Pharaoh himself when the Pharaoh was troubled by dreams of his own. Joseph told him what the dreams meant. As a reward, the Pharaoh made Joseph a great man in Egypt and elevated him to a place second only to the Pharaoh.

Years later, when famine came, Joseph's brothers came down from Canaan into Egypt to buy food. They were brought before the prime minister who, of course, was Joseph himself. The brothers did not recognize the little brother they had gotten rid of so meanly years before. After Joseph told them who he was, they all bowed low before him, just as his boyish dream said they would. They begged him to forgive them for the evil they had done and to spare their lives. His answer was: "You meant it for evil, but God meant it for good."

Joseph forgave his brothers. But his forgiveness did not mean that what his brothers did was not so bad after all, even though it had turned out fine for him. What they did to him was evil and will never be good if the world lasts forever. But good *did come* of the bad. And this is what Joseph chose to remember.

Forgiving does not edit bad things out of our memories anymore than it makes the bad things good. Forgiving only helps us remember the positive things that follow it.

We remember the past with truth.

When we forgive, we get new courage to recall what happened even though it wounded us badly and even though it was done by the ones in our lives we most trusted to do us good.

We also dare to recall our own responsibility for what happened to us, if we have any. In forgiving, we dare admit that we said yes to an abusive spouse when we really wanted to say no. That we supported his bad habits and made ourselves a target of his fury. Forgiving gives us eyes to see ourselves in truth for what we were and what we did to add to our pain.

We remember with a new respect for ourselves.

Victims often twist the wrong someone else did *to* them into something that is wrong with *them*. If someone abandons us, we imagine that we were not worth keeping. If someone abuses us, something bad in us must have made him do it. If someone we loved stops loving us, we must be unlovable.

But here is the saving irony. The way to restore our self-respect is to forgive the rotter who made us lose it. As we begin to forgive, we get the grit to aim the blame straight in the eyes of our culprit. And as we go on, we will heal the self-shaming memory and turn the experience of humiliation into a reason for pride. Nobody can ever do anything more worthy of self-respect than to break the grip of a painful past she never deserved and walk dangerously with hope into the possibility of tomorrow.

We remember with sadness.

Forgiving does not remove our scars any more than a funeral takes away all of our grief.

Not long ago I stood alone at the end of a small grave in Grand Rapids, Michigan, where our infant son was buried thirty years before. Now living in California, I had not visited the grave for some time, and the tears that this tiny piece of earth once sponged were long since dried. But as I stood there by myself, my old and almost forgotten grief percolated from my spirit as it did when we buried him. Where did this neglected, this long unnoticed grief come from? It came from the scars that stayed on the floor of my inner ocean after the waves of early grief had pulled back with the tide.

When we are wounded once, wounded and wronged, deeply wounded, sorely wronged, we carry a scar that stays when the wound is healed. If we are wounded in the fifth chapter of our story, we write the sixth chapter as a wounded author. When my grief rose from the grave, I was grateful to feel it again. It reconnected me with past chapters of my story and reminded me that, even though I am now writing another chapter, I am still the same person who wrote the grieving chapter.

It is so when a person forgives and the stitches are torn open by a remembrance of past wrongs. She can feel the healed pain again and be glad for the moment's connection with the past; it reminds her how good it is to be healed.

We remember without illusions.

Most of us enter marriage with two illusions. The first illusion is that the person we marry matches our fantasy of the partner we wanted. The second illusion is that if two people totally trust each other, their trust is itself security against breakage.

"I was so unbelievably dumb," the man said, "I thought that if we just trusted each other, we would never hurt each other. What a fool I've been." He was not a fool, but his trust in trust was an illusion. He simply believed that if someone puts enough trust in another person, that person will always honor the trust. When his wife violated his trust, his view of the world turned on its head, and he did not know how to get it right side up again.

To confuse trust with a guarantee is an illusion. His cheating wife punctured his illusion. Forgiving was his way of seeing his world without illusions and setting it back on its feet. With illusions dispelled, and the wound forgiven, he was ready for the alternative to illusion. He was ready for hope.

Illusions are fantasies of what cannot be. Hope is a faith in what can be. Illusions fantasize about guarantees. Hope is content with possibilities. Hope is based on a faith that lasting trust is possible, but not inevitable. Hope is the spirit's No to illusion and Yes to possibility.

When we forgive someone we change the course of a meandering river that could, if we let it, carry us on an aimless, endless current of remembered hurt and frustrated rage. We have changed our futures by as creative an act as any human being ever performs. Where will the river take us? Who can say? We cannot control the winding river we follow to our future any more than we could change the past. It will take us to places we can only imagine. It will take us to the possible goods for which we hope.

One way to lose hope for a better future is to be captive of a worse past. Nations lose hope, tribes lose hope, families lose hope, individuals lose hope when their visions of tomorrow are clouded by the wrongs of yesterday. One way to regain hope is to choose the new way of remembering that comes with forgiving the wrongs of the past.

∽

Forgiving is the only way to heal the wounds of a past we cannot change and cannot forget. Forgiving changes a bitter memory into a grateful memory, a cowardly memory into a courageous memory, an enslaved memory into a free memory. Forgiving restores a self-respect that someone killed. And, more than anything else, forgiving gives birth to hope for the future after our past illusions have been shattered.

When we forgive, we bring in light where there was darkness. We summon positives to replace negatives. We open the door to an unseen future that our painful past had shut. When we forgive, we take God's hand, walk through the door, and stroll into the possibilities that wait for us to make them real.

POSTSCRIPT: JUST REMEMBER THIS

The most creative power given to the human spirit is the power to heal the wounds of a past it cannot change.

We do our forgiving alone inside our hearts and minds; what happens to the people we forgive depends on them.

The first person to benefit from forgiving is the one who does it.

Forgiving happens in three stages: We rediscover the humanity of the person who wronged us, we surrender our right to get even, and we wish that person well.

We forgive people only for what they do, never for what they are.

We forgive people only for wounding and wronging us; we do not forgive people for things we do not blame them for.

We cannot forgive a wrong unless we first blame the person who wronged us.

Forgiving is a journey; the deeper the wound, the longer the journey.

Forgiving does not require us to reunite with the person who broke our trust.

We do not forgive because we are supposed to; we forgive when we are ready to be healed.

Waiting for someone to repent before we forgive is to surrender our future to the person who wronged us.

Forgiving is not a way to avoid pain but to heal pain.

Forgiving is done best when it is done intolerantly.

Forgiving someone who breaks a trust does not mean that we give him his job back.

Forgiving is the only way to be fair to ourselves.

Forgivers are not doormats; to forgive a person is not a signal that we are willing to put up with what he does.

We do not excuse the person we forgive; we blame the person we forgive.

Forgiving is essential; talking about it is optional.

When we forgive, we set a prisoner free and discover that the prisoner we set free is us.

When we forgive we walk in stride with the forgiving God.